THE EMPOWERED EDUCATOR

This book is dedicated to all my teachers, who may or may not have known their influence.

THE EMPOWERED EDUCATOR

10 Lessons to Prevent Burnout, Reclaim Your Joy, and Unlock Your Teaching Potential

JEN RAFFERTY, PhD

TARCHER
an imprint of Penguin Random House
New York

Tarcher
an imprint of Penguin Random House LLC
1745 Broadway, New York, NY 10019
penguinrandomhouse.com

Book design by Angie Boutin

Library of Congress Cataloging-in-Publication Data has been applied for.

Paperback ISBN: 9798217177967
eBook ISBN: 9798217177974

Printed in the United States of America
1st Printing

The authorized representative in the EU for product safety and compliance is Penguin Random House Ireland, Morrison Chambers, 32 Nassau Street, Dublin D02 YH68, Ireland, https://eu-contact.penguin.ie.

A teacher affects eternity;
he can never tell where his influence stops.

—HENRY ADAMS

CONTENTS

INTRODUCTION
FROM EXHAUSTED TO EMPOWERED

One of my favorite sayings is "Two opposing things can be true at the same time."

No one knows this more than teachers.

We absolutely love our jobs *and* we're so burnt out that a third of us will quit within our first five years in the classroom.[1]

We're passionate about educating kids *and* we're so overwhelmed with our workloads that we want to curl under our desks until the dismissal bell rings.

We want what's best for our students *and* we wish that someone would care about what's best for us.

Well, here comes another pair of truths.

Teachers are struggling to manage their stress *and* their lives would radically change for the better if they learned how.

I'm certainly proof of that.

For over fifteen years, I was a passionate, devoted music teacher in Central New York. As a child, I grew up believing that becoming an educator was how I was going to change the world. When I graduated from Ithaca College with my degree in music education, I couldn't wait to stand in front of a classroom filled with students. Like so many other teachers, my career became more than just a job. Being an educator became part of the fabric of who I was. I adored each of my students and gave them 110 percent of my attention. I thought I was holding up well under the pressure and scrutiny teachers are always subjected to.

Then came "Whitney-gate."

In my first few years, I always taught Whitney Houston's "Greatest Love of All" to my middle school choir students as a warm-up. Out of her *eleven* (!!!) number one singles, it's the one song most people can sing with confidence, so I created a simple arrangement that didn't require any vocal acrobatics. Plus, it's so inspiring. The lyrics alone could lift anyone out of a funk and make them believe they can do anything.

As it turns out, not all twelve-year-olds would agree with me. I'll never forget my sixth-grade student Maya yanking me away from my Yamaha piano for a one-on-one huddle in the back of the room amid all the filing cabinets of sheet music. A hush fell over the group as she not so gently delivered an important message.

"Ms. Rafferty, this song is hella cheesy," she said, her hands on her hips. "We took a vote and we all want to sing 'Teenage Dream' by Katy Perry."

Although this was clearly a mutiny, I tried to remain calm. "Um, I'll give that some thought."

I went back to my piano and started rifling through my sheet music. Then I felt this constricting sensation in my chest. It hurt to breathe. My hands were shaking like a leaf.

So I did what any other sensible teacher would do.

After class, I ran to the bathroom and hyperventilated in a toilet stall like a teenager who'd just been dumped.

This hadn't been the first time a conflict made me feel sick, panicked, or physically achy. Over the years, I started noticing my jaw would tighten whenever one of my students forgot their music folder at home or was late to class. My pulse would race at faculty meetings whenever the principal announced new plans, like adding more assemblies to our already packed schedules. At least once a week, I'd get nauseous on the ride to school because I was worried about any number of concerning things: district initiatives, state mandates, safety protocols, active shooter drills, laws about curriculum, not to mention the content I was actually supposed to teach.

Of course, my work angst followed me home. I was hanging on by a thread. (Although at the time I would rather have stepped on a LEGO brick than admit it.) Most afternoons when I left school, I was *so drained*. At night, I tried my best to rally and meaningfully connect with my family over quickly cooked dinners, but my efforts were often in vain.

To top it all off, I'd convinced myself that the answer to this problem was to act as if it didn't exist. I'd bought into these widespread (and ridiculous) stereotypes about teachers, like we're the Patron Saints of Indestructible Resilience, and nothing can deter or defeat us—including exhaustion, often-crippling anxiety, and seemingly endless stress. And this went on for years. While I was killing it at work, I was slowly killing myself. I was often sick, had bouts of debilitating back pain, and developed mysterious red splotches on my skin. On the outside, I was teacher of the year, but on the inside, I was a mess and afraid to admit it. The stress was overwhelming and became something I could no longer ignore. For years I was hiding in plain sight because I thought this was what the job required.

I know you can relate. Whether you're a new teacher who has just set foot on campus or someone like me, with more than a decade (or two) of teaching under your belt, we're all in the same boat . . . nervously waiting for it to capsize. We face a storm of challenges almost daily—everything from understaffing woes and scarce budgets to disciplinary issues and restrictions on what we can say in our own classrooms. We're not paid what our work is worth even though our expenses are skyrocketing year after year. We've been led to believe that we can mold and inspire young minds in a chaotic environment, as long as we don't stop to process the unrelenting stress and emotional triggers we endure.

The toll this is taking on educators can be heard in the troubling stories we whisper to one another behind closed doors. A friend of mine who's an elementary school teacher once admitted to wishing he'd catch COVID so he'd be forced to stay in bed and rest. Another teacher confided that when she got whiplash from a minor car accident, she was actually relieved. Finally she could take time off from work and do nothing but lie on the couch. And I'll never forget the teacher who shared that she'd told everyone she knew that her weeklong stay at the local hospital was due to appendicitis, but she'd really had kidney stones removed. Apparently for months she hadn't been drinking anything—no water, no coffee, *nothing*—all day because she didn't feel like she had enough time for a bathroom break during school hours.

You already know this, but I'll say it anyway.

None of this is okay.

Poor mental and physical health is *not* a part of a teacher's job description—or anyone else's, for that matter. Educators deserve *much* better than this, and so do our students. Our kids need us to be sturdy and grounded in order to become who they are meant to be.

Since our role as teachers is to lead by example, we have got to do just that. Because the truth is, the things that have contributed to the current culture can't magically change and make things right. Organizations don't change until *people* change, and the only person you have any agency in changing is yourself.

Yes, policies need to improve—sometimes drastically. Yes, we need to get the resources (and salaries) our work requires (and deserves). But what if we focused first on what we *can* control?

This is your agency. *This* is how you start to make change.

By building healthy self-awareness skills and breaking free from harmful patterns, we can manage our stress, regulate our emotions, and preserve our well-being. And that's just scratching the surface. We have the power to design a life for ourselves that is filled with abundance, ease, and joy. We can also pay forward what we've learned to our students and start a ripple effect of self-healing, self-love, and self-compassion that will be felt for years to come. We can not only *make* change but actually *be* the change—right here, right now.

I know this seems like a tall order. There is so much on your plate already. The thought of spending your minuscule amount of free time on another solution that makes big promises might not sound like fun. It might even feel like a waste of time.

Honestly, I've felt that way, too.

When I was in the classroom, I had days when I was convinced nothing would ever get any better. I had weeks when I felt defeated and hopeless. I bought book after book, program after program, trying to find something that would help. I sat in professional development days listening to "experts" (who rarely had a teaching background) give me advice on how to manage my life, while knowing virtually nothing about what educators go through for our students. I've heard all the well-meaning unrealistic suggestions from friends and family and left countless happy hours and dinner tables feeling misunderstood—even disrespected.

But we know this narrative needs to change.

That's why I wrote this book, and why you're reading it. You're ready for change.

Change can feel scary and overwhelming, but from here on out, you're not alone. You'll be joining a community of Empowered Educators who have seized their agency, altered their status quo, and started living lives that felt whole, balanced, grounded, and fulfilling. Supporting incredible teachers like you is my passion and the work of my heart. In 2021, I founded Empowered Educator—a company dedicated to helping teachers—because I saw how many teachers like me needed a lifeline. While there are groups and resources for struggling students, there is virtually no one teachers can rely on for sustainable respite and relief. I wanted to change that because my wish for you—and all 3.8 million educators in the United States—is that we stop living in survival mode and start feeling fully *alive.* Our kids need that from us. They're watching us.

I get that this might feel impossible now. But after doing this work, I've seen the shift happen for thousands of educators. And when it does, the result is inspiring, liberating, and truly exciting—for everyone.

Take Dolores, for example. As a special ed teacher, she was feeling completely depleted and numb, just going through the motions of her job. But what Dolores learned in Empowered Educator—also what you're going to learn in these pages—helped her to reconnect with her passion for teaching and showed her how to live with intention. Today Dolores shows up to work with joy in her heart and leaves school knowing she made a difference with her students. Then there's Cate, a new high school teacher who frequently had panic attacks because she was overwhelmed by the large class sizes at her school. After using the practices I'm going to share with you in this book, Cate advocated for herself and her students in a meeting with the principal. She presented a solution that would benefit her kids, and once it was implemented, her anxiety attacks went away. And finally there's Jin, a second-grade teacher, who was ashamed because he couldn't make it through a day without losing his temper. What he learned—what you can, too—was how to manage his feelings as they came up. As a result, Jin was proud to say that he felt patient and calm when dealing with even the most challenging students.

What I want you to know about Dolores, Cate, and Jin is that these results are just the beginning. Empowered Educator has created a paradigm-shifting grassroots movement among teachers that prioritizes our collective and individual well-being, recognizes our value, and celebrates the sheer awesomeness of what we do.

We already have the tools to make it happen.

We just need to learn the skills that will help us leverage them.

That's what this book is about. It's based on the work I do every day with teachers that shows us how to address our biggest pain points and reclaim agency in our lives. The stories, challenges, and wins I share here are all drawn from real working teachers just like you (though names have been changed and details have been blended). This is classroom tested. I've honed these principles over a number of years, and the teachers who have adopted them *love* that they're specially designed with educators in mind. This is not about making huge, sweeping changes or instituting some rigorous, overwhelming routine. Because what teacher has the time or the energy for that?

Instead, what you get to do to change your life is simple.

Read this book at your own pace and you'll be able to

breathe again. And by the end of the last chapter, you will have the road map to become an Empowered Educator:

- ✦ You'll have revitalized your mission and purpose as an educator and developed a clear vision for how you want to show up as a teacher.
- ✦ You'll be able to understand your thoughts and regulate your emotions.
- ✦ You'll have language that will help you advocate for yourself and your students.
- ✦ You'll have the tools to be physically, emotionally, and mentally healthy.

When I was able to apply what you're about to learn, I felt like there was nothing I couldn't handle. Even at the start of my journey, I was able to turn agonizing moments into teachable ones. Including Whitney-gate.

Thankfully, I didn't stay in the bathroom stall crying all day. After splashing some cool water on my face and looking in the mirror, I thought about why I was so shaken by Maya's challenging my song choice. I realized my sense of normalcy and control was being threatened. This song was the one constant in my classroom. The one thing I could hold on to when everything around me was always in flux.

But my song wasn't my students' song.

And that was more than okay. In fact, I realized that's how it's supposed to be.

Then I pictured Maya in her ripped jeans and high-top sneakers, looking me square in the eyes and being totally honest. At twelve years old, she was demonstrating more emotional intelligence than me (and let's face it, more than most of the other adults at school).

This child understood that she had the power to change her circumstances. She knew that talking to me and sharing how she felt would get her needs met. She discovered what she needed by tuning into her feelings and listening to them instead of shutting them out.

None of this was an accident. Maya learned how to be emotionally intelligent because someone—quite possibly another teacher—modeled this behavior for her. (Whoever did this, congrats on a job well done!) Maya picked up that behavior at such a young age. She was way ahead of the curve. Maybe she'd never have to excuse herself from a tough situation so she could go hide in the bathroom.

That's what flipped the switch for me.

I realized two things were simultaneously true.

My actions didn't affect just me and my well-being. They trickled down and helped my students learn how to conduct and respect themselves.

I knew that I had to go back into that music room and get it right.

The next day, my students looked worried, like they were going to be in trouble for making me upset. Maya was hunched over in her seat, her gaze glued to the floor. I stood in the center of the room, my body fully relaxed and my mind swimming with empowering thoughts.

You've got this. Change is good. This will be an exciting adventure.

"I'm glad you told me that 'Greatest Love of All' isn't your jam. I really value your input and want us to have fun in this class. Maybe we could think of a few other songs that are a bit more appropriate for the occasion and take another vote?"

The classroom erupted in cheers. The proud smile on Maya's face made my heart sing. What she'd done had made a difference. But there are thousands of kids—*our* kids—who don't know everything Maya does. And they might never learn if we don't *teach them well and let them lead the way*—just like Whitney said. (Couldn't help myself there!)

The only thing that's left for us to do is educate ourselves.

1

OPEN THE DOOR FOR CHANGE

On a particularly busy morning in the first few months of the school year, I heard a whisper inside my head.

"Sing, Jen. Sing."

This wasn't *entirely* out of the blue. I was a music teacher, the conductor of the school choirs, and a lifelong singer. I did (and do) love to sing, although at the time, other than singing with my students, I didn't have time to sing my own music outside of class. Nevertheless, I did what most people do when their inner voice surfaces: I ignored it.

Instead, I scrambled to pack up my stuff, rushed to make my kids breakfast, got them off to school, got *myself* off to school, and launched into a jam-packed day of instruction, faculty meetings, prep time (wherever I could squeeze it in), and after-school clubs.

I'd listen to the whisper when I had more time, I reasoned. Singing was going to have to wait.

Well, the whisper kept getting louder and louder until I just couldn't ignore it anymore. I hadn't taken a voice lesson since college, but I reached out to one of my former professors and scheduled a session. Since my graduation, Carol and I have kept in touch. We often exchange recommendations for TED talks we've watched (like Dr. Jill Bolte Taylor's) or interesting books we've read (one of our personal favorites: Brené Brown's *Atlas of the Heart*). Carol is brilliant and I'm always learning from her, whether it's about musical artistry or where to get the best quiche in Ithaca.

Still, I was really nervous about singing for her again—especially since I was showing up just because of a whisper in my mind.

At the start of the lesson, I sat at her piano and tried to sing "Back to Before" from the musical *Ragtime*, but I could barely make a noise. There was this strange pressure in my chest and my throat felt tight. Even though I'd sung this song a million times before, I was totally blocked. Then, with my fingers still on the keys, a wave of emotion overtook me. The tears were forming right behind my eyes, and I knew there was no holding back.

"Sing through it, Jen," Carol said.

I did. I kept playing and singing, even while my fingers shook and my voice trembled.

"That's okay," Carol said gently. "Keep going."

I sang on until suddenly I stopped singing and started sobbing. I'm talking head-in-my-hands, snot-bubbles-coming-out-of-my-nose *sobbing*.

I was overwhelmed. Not just by the strength of the emotions washing over me, but by the realization that I had no idea that my body and mind were so desperate for an emotional release. Maybe I'd been so busy trying to be Supermom and Teacher of the Year that I didn't notice I'd been neglecting myself. Maybe I'd been ignoring the physical signals that had been creeping up on me, like that tightness and pressure I felt when I actually tried to sing. But when I finally noticed what was inside me, when I let my body actually *feel* what it was clearly desperate to feel, it was like years of stress, grief, and pain were pouring out of me. And while I was wildly uncomfortable, the release felt necessary—good, even.

Once I composed myself, I felt lighter, like a weight I didn't even know I was carrying had been lifted off my shoulders. Carol encouraged me to keep going. So after a deep exhalation, I could finally sing my heart out.

Even though it felt scary at first, I'm glad I listened to that inner voice. I'm glad I opened myself up to that moment of vulnerability. I'm glad that I took the time to simply feel what I was feeling and express it in a real, meaningful way. And I'm glad I paid attention to what I needed.

As educators, we are intensely focused on the well-being of our students. We care deeply, we work hard, and we are the ultimate doers, forever juggling a hundred different tasks and making it look effortless. No wonder people often compare us to superheroes—even though that is, frankly, a dangerous narrative to internalize. (Teachers are heroes, definitely, but we aren't invincible—you never hear about Wonder Woman needing a mental health day.)

Yet even as we're taking on the world around us, showing up and turning out, supporting our students with whatever we can, we tend to neglect the world *within*. Too often we completely ignore our inner voice, that inner knowing that's trying to protect us from burnout, redirect us toward a good work-life blend, and reignite the passion that inspired us to become teachers in the first place.

As a result, we hold all this tension and stress inside. We soldier on in the classroom. We prep and plan in our "free" time. We sacrifice our sleep so we can grade tests and email frantic parents, and we show up the next day ready to roll.

But is that *really* what it looks like to show up as our best selves and to do our best work?

If my experience has taught me anything, the answer is a resounding no. Powering through a "random" headache that we've actually had for three weeks, surviving on iced coffee and protein bars, ignoring a worsening toothache because we can't find time to get to the dentist . . . none of this is showing up at our best. Not for our students, for our colleagues, or even for our friends, partners, and kids at home. (And certainly not for ourselves.)

You deserve more. And so do they.

The only way we can keep showing up for our kids day after day, engaged and committed, is to tend to our emotional needs. As counterintuitive as it sounds, the most generous thing you can do for the people in your life—your students, your fellow teachers, your family—is to *take care of yourself. Really* take care of yourself. By that, I don't mean the bubble bath, massage, get-your-nails-done one-off mental health day. I mean taking care of yourself through self-awareness, self-regulation, and emotional expression at the very *least*.

When that inner voice was telling me to sing, it wasn't just inviting me to do an activity I found fun and distracting. It wasn't about lifting my spirits or even finding time for myself (although music offers both of those). Somewhere, deep down beyond my conscious brain, that voice knew that my body, my physical self, was out of touch with the feelings brewing inside me. When you sing, though, you can't help but engage with your physical self. You need to breathe deeply. Engage your muscles for support *without* tensing up. Feel grounded and firm on your own two feet even if chaos is swirling around you. (In hindsight, even the song I chose—"Back to Before"—was a hint to myself!)

Without a doubt, we educators deserve to live from a place of peace, ease, and calm. Not just to preserve our own sanity, either. The school system is rife with problems; we all know it. But systems change from the inside out—when the people within them change. And the only person you genuinely have the power to change is yourself.

THE CLICHÉ THAT'S ACTUALLY TRUE: THE OXYGEN MASK PRINCIPLE

We all know that in-flight safety instruction: "Put on your own oxygen mask before helping others." You've heard it on planes, you've heard it in workshops, you've probably even read it in a few books before this one.

It's absolutely a cliché . . . and it's a powerful metaphor for what we need to remember as teachers. (Two things can be true at once, remember?):

Yes, I said as much earlier in the book, and I'll say it again now. I can't say it enough, honestly. As a teacher, as a *human,* you need oxygen, too. And you *can't* help other people—especially kids—to get what they need if you're holding your breath and powering through. Still not convinced? Imagine trying to exhale for ten minutes straight. Impossible, right? Your body isn't built for that. You have needs that require both giving (exhaling) and receiving (inhaling).

I'm going to be bold and say the quiet part out loud: Teachers are the very best humans. We signed up for the most important job in the world. We lay a foundation for every other career. We inspire curiosity. We ignite passion. We embolden creative thinkers. We foster a love of learning. (And that's just our day job!) So it's very natural that we want to spend all our time, our energy, our *everything* in making that happen for our students. But if we spend *all* of what we have and don't do the work to replenish it, then we're going to end up running on empty pretty quickly (and feeling out of breath, if you will).

Moreover, because of our deep commitment to this profession and our students, what we do becomes a part of our identity. But when we notice how teachers are praised and revered for being these compassionate martyrs, we start believing that our unlimited ability to give and sacrifice is actually what makes us special. We lose ourselves to our long list of job responsibilities and the high (and sometimes unrealistic) expectations of others. We assume that *to teach is to sacrifice ourselves and suffer*.

This means that often we simply don't think about shifting some of the energy that we spend helping others back to ourselves. Or if we do, it comes with a healthy side of what might be the most common disempowering emotion among teachers: *guilt*.

Teachers encounter guilt on the regular (amiright?).

When we take a real lunch break, we feel guilty for taking time for ourselves instead of teaching through it for students who need extra help, catching up on grading, or planning lessons.

When we go out for a short walk before or after school, we feel guilty for not spending that time on replying to parent emails or gathering data for our administrators.

When we short-circuit in front of our students because we are fed up with all our noninstructional duties, we feel guilty for taking our anger out on them.

While the guilt is understandable, it's also a choice (which we'll get to in depth later on). We start to believe that we're not worthy of love and care, that even things like taking a lunch break, eating healthy food throughout the day, or taking five minutes to go to the bathroom make us selfish or put our students at a disadvantage somehow.

Is any of this true? Of *course* not! Because remember: ***The most generous thing you can do for the people in your life, especially your students, is take care of yourself.***

It's the oxygen mask principle. To be anything, to *do* anything, you have to be breathing. To teach—and to teach well—you have to take care of yourself.

The bottom line is, our impact as teachers (and humans in general) is always going to be greater when we invest in ourselves. Putting more time, energy, resources, and attention into ourselves expands our capacity. When we become more emotionally and mentally available to everyone in our inner circle—our coworkers, students, families, and partners—we communicate more clearly and are more purposeful with our words and in our actions. We can deal with our stress and regulate our emotions so we have more energy and resilience when things are unpredictable (which, as every teacher knows, is every minute of the day).

Maybe this idea still feels totally radical. Maybe you know this is true intellectually, but you struggle to put it in practice in real life. Especially when the stakes are high, it's so easy to default to *help others* . . . and end up gasping for air. (And the stakes for us as teachers—or at least the pressures around us—are often high.)

That's okay. After all, we're just getting started here. For now, we can continue to look at what we're feeling with a sense of curiosity, so we can really see what's going on inside ourselves.

WHY EMOTIONS CAN FEEL SCARY

Humans aren't built for this high level of constant stress, and it takes a huge toll on teachers—whether we want to admit it or not.

For one thing, the educational system we work in, live in, and *breathe* in is on shaky ground. We teach in suboptimal conditions with not enough resources; our current kids are more anxious and depressed than the generation before them; every day there seems to be another budget cut, another contract dispute, or another discouraging news story about the state of education in our country.

On top of that, the world at large seems to be constantly in turmoil. Thanks to our smartphones and the ever-present social media, we have a front-row seat to every single local, national, and global crisis, twenty-four hours a day, school-related or otherwise.

We secretly break down whenever we're alone because the emotional onslaught we experience on the regular is much too great. Or we compartmentalize our feelings to the point where our bodies begin to succumb under the pressure. Maybe we even self-medicate with a bottle of wine or some gummies so we can be blissfully numb for a few hours. (No judgment here!)

I say all this not to complain about our situation, but to invite you to start by *giving yourself grace*. Whatever coping mechanisms you've developed to deal with your stress were created with good intentions. They all came from a place of protection and self-preservation. There is a tidal wave of uncomfortable feelings inside you—inside *all* of us. Reckoning with what is causing them can seem impossible, so we duck and run for cover. There is no shame in that at all. This is of course easy to say, but a totally different thing to take in. We are not broken or to blame for trying to power through the storm of emotions we're feeling and pretend that we're fine.

Because compounding the very real, very stressful state of things for teachers right now, most of us were never shown how to express or even acknowledge our emotions in a healthy and productive way. Our parents didn't have access to the tools or language to help us out—and neither did their parents or grandparents.

Thankfully, the tools are within our reach. Recent discoveries in neuroscience and psychology make it possible for us to teach ourselves these essential skills. By the end of this book, you'll have everything you need to navigate your emotions without fear or shame, as well as *regulate* them—rather than control, suppress, or ignore them—with ease.

Still, that doesn't mean that change doesn't feel scary—it very much can and often does. Moving through the world in a new, unfamiliar way can get all your physical systems sounding the alarm, making it feel incredibly uncomfortable.

I still remember the first (and only) snowboarding lesson I've ever had: One trip moving sideways down the hill with a slippery board strapped to my feet, and my body said NOPE. Turns out, I much prefer wearing cute earmuffs and drinking hot chocolate in the lodge, watching everyone else go down the hill.

By the same token, changing your habits (like suddenly moving sideways on a snowboard) isn't going to feel safe to your nervous system—at first. But unlike my attempt at snowboarding, your effort in this will earn you a lifetime of reward. Make no mistake: This takes work. But it's good work and important work—because it's work we're doing for more than ourselves.

We'll talk more in depth about why this is true in chapter 4, but I'll touch on it here because having some of this information now is important. *Any* change we make in our lives, whether it's trivial or major, is going to feel frightening on some level; our brains are hardwired to keep us alive and out of harm's way, and when we're trying something new, with *no* evidence yet that we can survive it, the conclusion our brain leaps to is DANGER! Even if what you're trying is something that is in your best interest.

So I'm here to tell you with 100 percent certainty: *You will survive exploring your emotions, even if it feels unfamiliar at first*. In fact, you're going to do more than just survive: You're going to adapt, rewire, grow, and *thrive*.

I know so many of us have made it this far in life suppressing and ignoring our feelings. We've been behaving like our house is a mess, and instead of tidying it up, we stuff all our belongings into a room. Over time as things accumulate, we won't let anyone enter that room, not even ourselves. Because we know if that door was ever opened, there would be a landslide, and everyone in its path would be buried in an instant.

But we aren't going to die from feeling our feelings, from going down that slippery, snowy hill faster than we're used to—even though our brain thinks we might (and my brain still isn't too sure about snowboarding). We can get our brains feeling safer as we process our emotions by remembering this simple truth: *Emotions are physical. Thoughts are mental.*

To illustrate what this looks like (and more important, *feels* like), here's a thought experiment.

Thought Experiment: A Dialogue with Your Body

These four short questions will help you paint the picture of what's happening physically in your body (which is where your feelings live). It's a great way to start tuning into the distress signals that your body is desperately trying to communicate to you, and that's the first step to decoding them and taking action. Grab something to write with to jot down some answers and go to *empowerededucator.com/book* for the resource.

QUESTION 1:
What are the sources of your stress right now?

Let's get real. We're teachers, so it's never just one thing causing us grief. It's usually a pile. We might be involved in a long-standing struggle with a student (or their parents) and haven't got the bandwidth to deal with it properly. We might be really behind in our lesson planning and can't find the time to catch up. Our car might need repairing, but our finances are a disaster right now. Or maybe our in-laws are coming to stay for the holidays and the house looks like someone has set off a keg of dynamite. Whatever combination of things it might be, jot down as many as you can for the next minute.

QUESTION 2:
What happens in your body when you think about those stressors?

When you started your list, how did your body feel? Did your stomach start to churn as you began mulling over your pain points? Or did you start getting a tension headache? After the minute was over, was your heart pounding or your shoulders tensing up? Now bring your attention to how your body feels when you're experiencing this stress in real time. Write about the impact on your body. Trouble sleeping? Extreme fatigue? Terrible diarrhea? (Hey, we've all been there.) Whatever symptoms you can think of, take a minute to acknowledge them. Our bodies talk to us all the time, but we tend to be terrible listeners. Physical symptoms are the *only* means our body has to communicate with us, and unfortunately we usually ignore these signs. Now let's go deeper with the next question.

QUESTION 3:
How do you show up for others when under stress?

Do you snap at your partner? Lose your temper with your kids? Find yourself feeling impatient with your students? Forget to make that phone call, pay that bill, pick up that prescription, or even text back that friend?

Or maybe you just seclude yourself, collapse into bed, and doomscroll for hours . . . failing to get the sleep you so desperately need.

Take a minute to write down how you act when you're physically carrying the weight of this stress. It can be short, descriptive sentences like these: "I am impatient with my colleagues." "I am rude to my students." "I am exhausted and not present." "I am distracted."

QUESTION 4:
What would happen months or years from now if you continue to ignore the messages your body is screaming at you?

Yeah, this is usually the big "oh, shit" moment teachers have during this experiment. It's almost too easy to draw the connection between our body's symptoms in the here and now and the eventual outcome if we keep tamping them down.

So what kind of chain reaction or worst-case scenario do you picture? Maybe we develop a very serious chronic illness that keeps us bedbound, or have a panic attack at school. (Honestly, I've lost track of the number of teachers who have told me that they've had some sort of cardiac event because of a stress-related situation at work.) Maybe our relationships deteriorate. There's built-up conflict with our partner, or our kids are acting out at home, because we're not emotionally present enough. We can also think about quick fixes that we've tried, like self-medicating with alcohol, sugar, or social media. What does your future look like if that behavior continues? Spend a minute writing those possible outcomes down.

Let's just take a moment and validate some of what might have come up for you in this thought experiment. There is nothing wrong with you: You're not broken, you don't need to be fixed, *and* you get to make a decision here. Are you going to continue down this path or decide to live differently? Let's stop counting down days until Friday, weeks until summer vacation, or years until retirement, so you can finally feel good. Because the truth is, retirement is not guaranteed. So what are we waiting for? What are we actually doing and what are we teaching our kids? (Again, our kids are watching us.) It's time you get to decide to live your life by design instead of by default.

So take a moment and pause before we learn how to shift from feeling emotionally exhausted to feeling regulated and empowered.

Remember to breathe—you got this.

EMOTIONAL REGULATION: CALMING THE CASTLE GUARD

Now that we know that *emotions are physical* and *thoughts are mental*, it's tempting to assume that we just need to think to ourselves, *You're okay! Stop being afraid!* and our brains will fall in line. However, that's not quite how the whole system works—it's kind of the opposite, in fact. (I mean, when was the last time someone told you to calm down and it actually worked?) Rather than conscious thoughts informing our bodies how to react, *emotions are physical* because our brain's threat-detection system is so fine-tuned and efficient that it can kick our bodies into gear without a single thought ever registering consciously in our minds. Threat detection often happens subconsciously.

You can think of your brain's threat-detection system like a subconscious castle guard patrolling the walls (more on the science in chapter 4). Good castle guards aren't relaxed and chill and go with the flow, right? They're on high alert, 24/7, keeping an eye out for attackers. They have the crossbows and vats of boiling water ready to go at a moment's notice. It doesn't matter if that flicker of motion in the distance is a charging enemy cavalry or just a branch twisting in the wind—they're going to jump into action either way, *just in case.* Better safe than sorry.

The same way that castle guard keeps all their weapons at the ready, your brain's threat-detection system—when it's on high alert from all the stressors you identified—keeps your *body's* defenses locked and loaded. This can look (and feel) like muscle tension (so you're ready to jump out of the way), a racing heart and quick, shallow breathing (so you're ready to run), and even a churning stomach (digesting quickly, rather than efficiently, so your body isn't wasting resources on breaking down nutrients).

In theory, this is a good thing. For generations of humans, those flickers of motion (aka stressors) more often than not meant a predator or a natural disaster was coming to take us down, so keeping our bodies on edge was what kept us alive. But nowadays—when we're more likely to face down a condescending school board member than a saber-toothed tiger—our castle guard is *way* overcompensating. In fact, many of us don't know *what* our castle guard is reacting to, let alone how to talk them down when they are pacing all day and night.

Calming down that castle guard—aka regulating our nervous system—starts with dismantling some of those physical defenses (it's much easier to talk down jumpy castle guards when they're *not* aiming a crossbow at your face, after all). And *that* starts with simply noticing when those feelings (both physical and emotional) arise in us.

Regulating your nervous system is a huge, important, life-changing skill. It's what will help you work toward cultivating a sense of awareness *and* groundedness that allows you to respond, rather than react, to the stressors in your life. It'll calm your body so you can explore your emotions with curiosity and self-compassion, not judgment. It'll form the foundation of pretty much everything you'll undertake on this journey through these chapters.

So give yourself permission to try some self-regulation, even if you still feel that resistance. Change requires patience, grace, and an openness to trying new things *and* recommitting to trying again. If an exercise doesn't work right away, that's normal—your castle guard has been on patrol for *years*. Also, each nervous system is as unique as a fingerprint—what works well for me might not work well for you, and vice versa, so explore these exercises through the lens of playful experimentation and keep track of the ones that feel good in your body.

Exercise: Cleansing Breath

This exercise is an excellent self-regulation technique to keep in your back pocket. Your breath is portable, simple, and always present with you. These cleansing breaths allow you to let go of any tension you might feel in your body and give yourself the space to relax completely: Deep, steady breathing does wonders to calm down the threat-alert system in your body by slowing your pulse. In order to dial down the stimuli that might be activating that castle guard, you can also try finding a quiet place and closing your eyes.

Wherever you are, inhale twice through your nose and then have a long, deep exhale. Repeat this three times in a row. The longer exhale of this breath helps release trapped carbon dioxide and allows for a greater oxygen exchange. It can also reduce tightness in your shoulders, chest, or jaw.

Exercise: Quick Body Check-in

If you can, find a quiet place where you can sit down (or lie down) comfortably. Start by taking a nice, intentional breath deep into your body. As you breathe, bring your awareness to your abdomen, noticing how it expands on the inhale and contracts on the exhale.

Now breathe in again with the awareness on your belly, following the rise and the fall and guided by the breath: inhale expand, exhale contract.

On the next breath, gently bring your attention to your ribs. Notice how they expand outward on the inhale and back in again on the exhale. Breathe in once more and continue being aware of how your ribs expand and contract. Follow the breath from your abdomen and up through your ribs: Breathe in, expanding your abdomen and your rib cage, and breathe out again, contracting, almost as if this is a breath in two phases.

Take as many breaths as you need. If it feels comfortable, try this exercise with your gaze lowered or your eyes closed. Revisit this body check-in as often as you need.

Exercise: The Box Breath

This breathing exercise has four equal stages—like the sides of a box.

Inhale for a count of four, pause for a count of four, exhale for a count of four, pause for a count of four. Repeat three times.

Here's an optional variation that can be even more grounding: Put one hand on your heart and the other on your stomach so you can feel the air move in and out.

EMBRACE YOUR INNER NANCY DREW: GETTING CURIOUS ABOUT THE FEELINGS YOU'RE FEELING

Melissa, a forty-two-year-old third-grade teacher in Houston, Texas, attended one of my professional development sessions where we went through the thought experiments and exercises in this chapter. After we were done, she said, "That was amazing. I feel like the Nancy Drew of my emotions right now!" The room laughed, of course, but I thought she hit the nail right on the head.

Once we open the communication channel with our bodies, we really do transform into detectives. The same way Nancy Drew investigated mysteries and pieced together clues in pursuit of the whole picture, we get to be observant, looking for hints in our body, and then attempt to connect them with emotions lying beneath the surface.

With this perspective in hand, Melissa went back to her school ready to investigate. She had a theory that the flare-ups of her autoimmune disease were work-stress-related. So as the school year started, Melissa started journaling, noting her emotional state and her physical symptoms. For the first few weeks, she felt pretty good . . . and then it came time to prepare her students for upcoming state assessments.

Suddenly her symptoms emerged in full force. Her joints and muscles ached mercilessly. Her stomach was in constant knots. She missed several days of work, and her worry that her students would fall behind made her incredibly anxious. After the testing period was over, Melissa thought she would feel a little better. But surprisingly, she felt worse, and this lasted for weeks. The fatigue was nearly debilitating. Her skin was constantly red and itchy. She had more absences, too.

Melissa was feeling defeated but then remembered to get curious and unlock her inner Nancy Drew. Instead of getting down on herself for not feeling well, she understood that there were some deep-seated feelings that were desperately trying to break through, and these symptoms were her body's only way of communicating with her. The cause of the stress that she suspected triggered an autoimmune reaction appeared to be the state testing. The fact that she didn't begin to feel better once the tests were over was another clue.

The feelings Melissa uncovered are difficult to face. But I'm going to put this next point in bold and italics because I want you to take this to heart.

Just because some feelings are uncomfortable, that doesn't make them bad.

We are so fortunate to be able to feel the full range of emotions. After all, that's what makes us human! And truthfully, we can't feel emotions like love, pride, happiness, and peace to their fullest unless we experience emotions like grief, depression, anger, resentment, and frustration, too. We can't just cherry-pick the emotions that feel good. We get to feel them all.

Unfortunately, most of us have internalized the idea that some feelings are positive and others are negative. And based on *that* belief, we also believe that if we're experiencing what we consider to be a negative feeling, there must be something wrong with us. Or our response is "Ugh! I hate feeling this way—how can I get out of this state ASAP?"

Although this belief is ingrained in our psyche, we can root it out if we reframe it. Instead of thinking of emotions as good and bad, we can recast them as *empowering* and *disempowering.*

What this mental shift does is remove the blame, shame, and judgment, making our feelings more neutral. True, *disempowering* isn't exactly an upbeat descriptor, but—crucially—it's merely describing the impact these kinds of feelings have on us. It's not a value judgment one way or the other, positive or negative.

Through her journaling, Melissa realized that when she was honest with herself, the testing period brought up strong feelings of insecurity and doubt. Whenever her students received low scores, Melissa felt terrible and berated herself. Clearly she was an ineffective teacher and had no business leading a classroom anymore. When her students did well, it almost felt like she got lucky.

These feelings of insecurity and self-doubt didn't make her a bad teacher (or a bad person). However, they were disempowering in two ways: They aggravated her condition and kept her away from her classroom, where she was needed and wanted to be.

So forget the preconceived notions that our feelings have

morality baked into them and they define who we are. They don't. Our emotions, when we honor them, are a gift of self-discovery and wisdom. They are all indicators that either we are right on track or something is off and requires our attention. They are inviting us to investigate and look deeper within ourselves so we can discover our truth and make different choices. Remember, like Nancy Drew, you're simply investigating—not judging.

Over the next few months, Melissa started to unpack where her insecurities were stemming from. By the next school year, when testing season came around, she noticed her health didn't seem to be triggered by the usual stressors, in part because her belief had entirely changed. Her mantra became, *The outcome of these tests does not dictate my self-worth.*

Exercise: Stop and Notice

This stress management technique helps us be more self-aware by slowing down and paying attention to our feelings, which we now know are firmly rooted in our body. This might seem easy in theory, but since we are used to being in a constant state of hustle and productivity, it can actually feel a little challenging.

This exercise is as simple as its name. First, put your hand on your heart. This will help ground you in your body. Now do one of the breathing exercises from earlier in this chapter. (My go-to is usually the box breath.)

It's time to start noticing. Take a quick inventory of anything you might be feeling physically. For instance, if your stomach is clenched or you notice that your shoulders are up to your ears, that's another opportunity for investigation. You might ask yourself, *What was I thinking about before I stopped to check in? Was I dreading that meeting with an administrator? I skipped breakfast, so am I just hungry?*

These might seem like elementary questions, but they are foundational for having that conversation with your body. Consider this: When we were babies, all we had was our physiological responses to tell us and our caregivers that our needs weren't being met. We just had our instincts and our bodies—that's it! As we age, we tend to disregard the same instincts and inner knowing we once relied on for our survival. There are many, many reasons this can happen (they could fill a book of their own). Regardless of the root causes, the distrust of our bodies has become subconscious, so we don't even know we're doing it.

That's why this technique can be incredibly useful—it intentionally interrupts the multiple hamster wheels that we're on and forces us to be still, clear the mind, and take stock. For example, a teacher once told me Stop and Notice helped her realize that she dreaded interacting with a fellow teacher. Her mornings would go just fine, but once she was approaching her lunch, her pulse would start racing and her stomach would knot up.

When she noticed that this was happening regularly, she realized her body was trying to communicate with her and tried to figure out what was going on. Ultimately, she understood the panic she felt while heading for the teachers' lounge for a bite to eat was because that's where she was usually cornered by a gossipy coworker. She felt sure that if she hadn't tuned into her body, it would have taken her much longer to recognize this pattern and come to the conclusion that she needed to set a no-gossip boundary with her colleague (more on that in chapter 7).

I recommend taking four moments during the school day to briefly put life on pause and Stop and Notice, specifically:

Before you walk on campus. If you drive, sit in your parked car. If you take public transport or catch a lift another way, you can do it on your commute.

During lunch break. If you find yourself in the teachers' lounge, in an empty classroom, or even in the bathroom, that's a great spot for this. (And if you don't take lunch, that's a separate conversation we'll have in another chapter!)

Post-dismissal. Similar approach to the before-arrival pause.

In the evening. Sometime before dinner or before you go to bed.

Practicing regularly is how you start to build a sense of *trust* in those signals your body is sending—and that trust is transformative. The more trust we put in ourselves and the more we believe that our bodies are telling us something we need to hear, the more we choose something other than the conditioning and disempowering feelings that keep us detached, dysregulated, and chasing our own tails—and make us less impactful as teachers.

This sense of trust is what's going to carry us through this whole process of becoming fully empowered as educators, one step at a time. (You can grab a PDF of this exercise at *empowerededucator.com/book* to take with you and share, too.)

THE TRUTH ABOUT CRYING

I want to take a moment to promise you that if getting in touch with your emotions elicits tears (or the head-in-your-hands, snot-bubbles-coming-out-of-your-nose *sobbing* that I described earlier in this chapter), there's nothing wrong with you—and you also aren't alone. Seriously, you wouldn't believe how many teachers are worried that once those emotional floodgates open, they are done for. Maybe we assume that crying is immature, so we tell ourselves that adults aren't supposed to be weak and vulnerable. Maybe we've learned from years of hearing "Stop crying—I'll give you something to cry about!" that our feelings are inconvenient, even harmful, to the people around us. We have to keep it together, because if we don't, there's something wrong with us.

I'll say it again: There is *nothing wrong with you.* You are beautifully *human.* Crying is simply a physical release of unprocessed emotion. (Kids seem to have received the memo, but somehow we haven't!) The only reason it has meaning is because we impose meaning on it. And the more we try to fight off the tears, the more we betray ourselves and therefore our students, who need us to be authentic, genuine, responsive humans, not emotionless robots. Crying is another way to process an emotion, and that is *always* healthy. (Of course, use discernment to decide what spaces feel safe to process that emotion. If you don't have a space to feel safe, create one for yourself.)

HOW DO YOU WANT TO FEEL?

At the end of the day, this work on our emotional well-being is about the responsibility we have to our students and everyone around us. As teachers, we've stepped into this role to pave the way for the next generation. In the classroom, we've made social-emotional learning a priority—for them (which is obviously important). But we've been leapfrogging over our emotional needs for far too long, and we're not showing up for our students in the way they need. Sacrificing our emotional health is unsustainable. It's not good for us, and it's not good for our students. And from here on out, it's a thing of the past.

So imagine that you can choose how you feel every day the same way you choose what you want to wear. What do you want your mood to be like when you wake up in the morning? How about when you first walk into your classroom? What about in a faculty meeting or in a difficult interaction with a student? How do you want to feel in those situations?

We often focus on how we *don't* want to feel. We want to stop feeling stressed, frustrated, and overwhelmed. But the more attention we pay to the difficulties we're experiencing, ironically the less motivated we are to do something about it (more on that in chapter 4).

So as you're getting in touch with what you're feeling, listening to your body's signals, and starting to process what comes up, here's another opportunity to do something: *Decide how you want to feel.*

A big part of the work in this book will essentially be making room for who you want to become. Yes, that means letting go of habits, actions, and ideas that no longer serve you. But it also means choosing what you want to take in.

To move toward a new, empowered state of being, we have to know what we want that new state to feel like.

So ask yourself: What feelings do you want in your life? Maybe you decide *I want to feel excited when I see my students* or *I want to feel inspired after a faculty meeting* or just *I want to wake up full of energy every day*. Take your time with this. Dig deep and think broadly and boldly. This isn't "think happy thoughts until you feel better." This isn't about bypassing any emotions that are uncomfortable so you can skip to the good part. This is about laying a foundation to be crystal clear about what you want (instead of what you don't want) so you can build on it in the upcoming chapters. If you'd like some inspiration to get you started, go to *empowerededucator.com/book* for an empowering emotions word bank.

MAIN TAKEAWAYS

- Emotional expression starts with building self-awareness and strengthening our attentiveness. You can't change something you don't notice.
- Emotions are felt in the body because our nervous system uses our body's defenses to try and keep us safe.
- Our emotions are indicators that provide useful information about how our nervous system is sizing up the situation we're currently in based on past experiences. (They are not proof that we are a good or a bad person!)
- Physical symptoms (like tense muscles or a racing heart, for example) signal that we need to investigate what's going on.

2

RENEW YOUR PASSION FOR TEACHING

During one of my recent workshops in upstate New York, Farrah, a veteran educator with a wealth of experience, confessed something that sent shock waves through the room.

"Recently I feel like I don't know what I'm doing. Every day, it's like I'm a first-year teacher."

Farrah was known for being exceptional at her job. She connected with her fourth-grade students, who all seemed attentive and eager to learn from her. She got along well with her fellow teachers, the administrators, and the parents, and she never seemed to miss a beat.

So it's no wonder her colleagues' eyes widened with surprise as she went on to describe how bad she was feeling inside.

Depleted. Stressed out. Confused. Uninspired. And just . . . *lost*.

Like she was a first-year teacher and didn't know what she was doing.

When I think back to what it felt like to be a first-year teacher, quite frankly? It was *hard*. You're brand-new in a job with a learning curve that's steeper than the Grand Canyon. You're simultaneously running a classroom, trying not to screw up school procedures, creating lesson plans that are challenging yet engaging, and teaching your content for the first time to students you're just getting to know. It can take a whole school year to develop organizational systems and routines to help you manage everything. Even then you can still feel like you've tumbled into a dark hole that you can't see a way out of.

But Farrah *wasn't* a first-year teacher anymore. She had been at this for a long time. How was she *still* feeling this lost and disoriented? Why wasn't it getting any easier?

True, she appeared to be managing everything well at school. Behind the scenes, though, she was barely getting from one dismissal bell to the next.

I'm sure you've felt like Farrah more than once in your teaching career. There is just *so much* to tackle and triage every day at school. That list of teaching responsibilities is only scratching the surface. You put maximum effort into each thing you do, including the minutiae, and exhaust yourself in the process. You tell yourself if you scale back in the slightest, you won't measure up or will fall too far behind. So you push yourself harder. You try to do everything and be everywhere all at once. As a result, the hole you feel like you're in gets deeper and deeper.

Feeling helpless like this can be paralyzing. You need a lifeline. A flashlight to enable you to see in the dark. Something to grab on to so you can pull yourself up. And part of that saving grace is connecting with something bigger than the situation in front of you.

It's your philosophy as an educator. It's the bedrock of how you teach in the classroom. It's the driving force behind your work—the inspiring spark that gets you out of bed in the morning, excited to mold young minds. It's the reason you put so much thoughtful care into preparing your content and listening to your students' problems. This force is your mission, your *why*.

I know you've heard the catchphrase "Remember your why" a million times, and your eyes are probably rolling now because you think you know where this is going. So many self-help experts and leadership gurus have been trotting that saying out in their books. Professional development speakers have done the same thing in their talks. I totally get that you might feel tired of it. Honestly, it can feel pretty patronizing to hear those words when we're feeling stuck or frustrated. You can't just "remember your why" out of a stressful situation. Remembering why you began a task or started a project or chose a career doesn't always lead to a breakthrough, especially if not examined in the right way. (In fact, sometimes it can lead to resentment—quite the disempowering emotion.)

So instead of just *remembering* your why, you're going to start *living* it.

Living your mission means actively putting your why at the center of everything you do as an educator—and once you do that, everything changes. You have a sharp, laser-like focus because you know which parts of your job align with your why and which parts don't. You have more energy and confidence because you're reserving most of your time and attention for the things that support your mission. You can set boundaries with ease because you're clear on what behaviors and interactions are in service of your why and which aren't. You feel stronger and calmer at the same time. You're certain instead of confused. Determined instead of listless. Empowered instead of defeated.

So whether you've forgotten your mission due to (A) anxiety from the massive mental load you are carrying at work; (B) overwhelm from juggling a hundred tasks at once; (C) depression resulting from the chaotic state of the world; or (D) all of the above, you're going to rediscover what it—and your work—is all about. You'll revisit your inspiration, learn how to start showing up with intention, and take steps to prioritize things that fall into alignment as a way to reduce your stress levels *and* expand your impact as a teacher.

When you do, I promise you're going to have the clarity and precision of thought needed to stop spinning your wheels and move forward with purpose again.

YOU AREN'T *JUST* WHAT YOU DO

One thing I want to be clear about before we move on: Your mission as an educator is not your life's purpose. While your mission can certainly align with who you are and what your values are, your life has many more and varied purposes beyond your job as an educator. So as we navigate this chapter, remember to hold space for who you are *out* of the classroom, too. More about that in chapter 5.

INSPIRATION: THE FIRE INSIDE

You didn't become a teacher by accident.

You made choices that led you in this direction. You chose

the profession, carefully picked the right college, made decisions about what you wanted to teach and to whom you wanted to teach it, and you probably chose to spend a significant amount of time and money for your degrees. In fact, you are probably still paying some of those student loans back even now. (I know I am, at least!)

But have you stopped to think recently about what feelings, hopes, and dreams were at the root of all these decisions? What about the people in your life who influenced you to make some of those choices—how did they impact your decisions? What about where you grew up, or even where you went to school as a kid? Did that play a significant role in why you became a teacher?

Whether you're feeling out of touch with your mission, or you aren't clear on what your mission even is in the first place, the best way to (re)connect with it is by figuring out what your *inspirations* are.

Now, in the education world, *inspiration* can sometimes be confused with *motivation.* We teachers love using rewards to tap into our students' immediate desires and encourage them to reach a goal. My kids have brought home plenty of little prizes from school as a reward for completing classroom contests designed to boost interest in certain subjects. In fact, I *still* remember being in third grade and screaming with delight when our class won a pizza party for reading the most books all year.

Motivations and incentives like this can seem to work wonders with kids and move the needle with their efforts. But inspiring them to rise to a challenge without tempting them with something shiny and yummy can be much harder, right?

That's because true inspiration runs much deeper.

Inspiration is what fuels your desires. It spurs you into taking action, regardless of whether there's a reward on the horizon. Inspiration keeps you going over the long haul, when times are hard and things aren't going well.

Inspiration *moves* you. No matter what the circumstances are.

You can think about the relationship between *mission* and *inspiration* as being like a hot air balloon: Your mission is the balloon itself, and your inspiration is the fire that comes out of the burner. When that fire is blazing, the air inside the balloon becomes warmer than the air on the outside and the balloon begins to float upward, higher and higher. When the fire's dwindling (or has gone out entirely), the balloon doesn't go anywhere.

If you feel like your fire is out right now, that's understandable. Your inspiration at the moment might be just to move from one class to the next without collapsing from stress and exhaustion. I see you. However, finding your fire again is up to you. (Honestly, you probably already know that, because otherwise you wouldn't have picked up this book!)

So here is your first mission-discovery tool that will rekindle your inspiration and lift you back off the ground.

Thought Experiment: Your Teaching Origin Story

This visualization exercise takes you back to the early days of your teaching journey and reminds you why you became a teacher in the first place. This will help you get to the heart of your inspiration and grab hold of your mission again. Take some time in a quiet space with something to write down your thoughts. (You can also download a printable PDF version at *empowerededucator.com/book*.)

Start by thinking back to when you first considered becoming a teacher. Let your mind wander around a bit until it arrives at the point when you were contemplating making this your career. Once you're there, take a deep inhalation, followed by a long exhalation, and try to remain locked in.

Now begin to let the details of the picture take shape in your mind's eye. Observe yourself and your surroundings like a fly on the wall. Are you in a college lecture hall, listening intently? Or are you a student in the classroom with your favorite teacher? Maybe you're in your childhood bedroom playing school with your dolls or your siblings, or maybe you're with a teacher who is helping you through a tricky situation.

Jot down as much as you can "see" around you, especially who's there at your side, and focus on how you felt at that moment. Let the images from your memories become emotional touchpoints. Allow them to light up in front of you and write down those feelings.

This moment (or moments) in your life was when you realized that becoming a teacher was a career you wanted to pursue. Why? What moved you inside to see that possibility and want to go for it? Write down anything and everything that comes to mind.

Once you've pinned down your why, write as many details as you can recall about what was inspiring you then. Again, how were you feeling? What were you anticipating feeling when you became a teacher? Take all the time you need here; we're going to come back to these emotions later in this chapter. (And if you find any part of this exercise challenging, that's okay! When you draw a blank, simply step away and try again when you're ready.) For me, I distinctly remember being in choir, singing with my favorite teacher, Mr. Williams, who always met us with unfiltered enthusiasm. I consistently remember thinking, *That is what I want to do. I want to inspire people to find their voice,* which is why I became a music teacher.

INTENTION: THE PROMISE YOU MAKE TO YOURSELF

Whether Farrah—the teacher who confessed to feeling overwhelmed and lost—meant to or not, she started a trend in our workshop that day. Once she spoke up, a handful of other teachers began sharing their biggest pain points at their jobs. Student behavior. Academic gaps and differentiation. Lack of emotional and mental health support. And so much more.

All of them said they were on the verge of burnout.

Phil, a middle-school English teacher, pulled no punches. He stood up and went off on school administrators who were overloading him with "bullshit busywork" that they wanted completed on unreasonable timelines. He put some parents on full blast because they were repeatedly emailing him with push-back on student behavior, then complained when he didn't respond quickly enough. He even pointed the finger at his own students for their lack of engagement in his class.

"If I'm not making learning fun every minute, they either zone out or act out," Phil said. "Teaching has become even more thankless."

I could tell by their stiff, uncomfortable body language that certain people in the room were just waiting for Phil to continue to pop off with his list of gripes. Some of them seemed to view him as the aggravating squeaky wheel/employee that every principal and colleague wish would pipe down about whatever is bothering them, because something is bothering them *all the time*. Many of them also agreed with Phil—teaching has changed.

But I could see past Phil's outrage to the weariness in his slumped shoulders and in his strained voice. To me, his rant seemed less like a squeaky wheel and more like a security alarm going off. It was like he was trying to tell everyone that he was in distress and desperately needed some help.

Thankfully, Farrah caught onto this vibe, too, and backed him up. "I understand where Phil is coming from. We're all putting 100 percent of our effort into everything, 100 percent of the time. That's just bad math."

Logically speaking, this was true: No, it does not compute. But there was also something else going on here.

I was paying close attention to what Phil was saying, and a lot of his dissatisfaction was based on what other people were expecting from him. He thought it was unfair for his administrators to expect him to drop everything he was doing and switch to a new curriculum this year. He believed it was unkind for parents to question his teaching methods and then expect him to respond to them within a day. He felt bad that he didn't have the energy to be Mr. Excitement in the classroom.

Trying to meet every single expectation from every member of the school community was making Phil tired and bitter, especially because his expectations about being recognized for his hard work weren't being met, either. It was affecting his ability to do his job well and feel that he was making a difference.

At the same time, there was so much Phil *couldn't* change. He couldn't change the expectations of his principals, he couldn't change the reactions from parents, and he couldn't change his students' choices.

But what he *could* do is choose how he was showing up to all the things he couldn't control. *That* is agency. He could notice how he's feeling, regulate his emotions (rather than push them down), and start teaching with intention—which is another vital part of living your mission.

Your intentions are your personal focus. They are the

promises you make to yourself to guide your actions. And defining and aligning with those intentions—not with others' expectations—are what will make you truly impactful in your work.

Now, since I have been in the classroom for almost two decades, I can tell you that many of us have overachieving, people-pleasing, perfectionistic tendencies, and the thought of *not* meeting the expectations of administrators, colleagues, and parents can make our skin crawl. Teachers don't want to disappoint anyone. We don't want to let anyone down. We certainly don't want to miss the mark on any standards and requirements.

In this context, however, letting go of expectations in favor of intentions is more about exercising discretion. Where we so often run into trouble is in treating *all* expectations as equally important, assuming we have to give all of them 110 percent and run ourselves into the ground doing so. It's the forty-five extra minutes we spend laboring over our bulletin board to make sure it matches the other teachers' displays. It's making sure we never, *ever* miss a faculty meeting . . . even if we have an urgent dentist appointment. It's always responding to parent emails in under twelve hours, no matter when they hit our inbox. That leaves us drained and stressed, feeling like we can never do what matters to *us*—the things that inspired us to become a teacher in the first place.

But when you can make this perspective change, letting your *intention* guide you instead of the *expectations* of others, you'll become the teacher who walks into the classroom self-assured, full of energy, and grounded in what truly matters to you. You'll meet and exceed your teaching responsibilities with more satisfaction and grace. Your students will get the benefit of being taught by someone who isn't frayed at the edges or going from class to class, simultaneously bewildered and frantic.

So in order for you to figure out what your intention is as

an educator and commit to it, here's another thought experiment called **Why × 5.**

Thought Experiment: Why × 5

This question-asking experiment is a great way to drill down to the core of your intentions by returning to one single word: *why.* Journal on this, or download the printable PDF at *empowered educator.com/book.*

WHY #1:
Why did I become a teacher?

Yes, you answered this question in your Teaching Origin Story, so go back to your notes and summarize your thoughts into one sentence that begins with "I became a teacher because . . ." That is your shorthand response to this first why.

Here are Farrah's and Phil's answers.

Farrah: *I became a teacher because I wanted to be that one constant positive person in children's lives.*

Phil: *I became a teacher because I wanted kids to love going to school.*

Once you've written a sentence you feel comfortable with, you can move on to the next why.

WHY #2:
Why is that important to you?

By thinking more deeply and critically about the importance of your first why, you become much more aware of your true inspirations. Try to answer quickly, without analyzing too much, so your response is more instinctual.

For reference, Phil's answer to Why #2 was: *Kids loving school is important to me because it makes their learning environment more comfortable.* Farrah's second answer was: *Being a constant positive person in children's lives matters to me because it helps them feel emotionally safe.*

WHY #3:
Why is Why #2 important to you?

Now that you're going a little bit deeper, what you value most as an educator is going to start rising to the surface. You can spend a little more time on this one, but don't overthink it.

Phil's Why #3: *A comfortable learning environment is important to me because it makes learning so much easier for students.*

Farrah's Why #3: *Feeling emotionally safe is important to me because it helps build trust between me and my students.*

WHY #4:
Why is Why #3 important to you?

This is the tipping point where your exploration can get a bit more personal and touch upon some pivotal life moments.

As for Phil and Farrah, here's what they had to say:

Phil: *Making learning easier is important to me because I struggled with my academics as a student and it hurt my self-esteem.*

Farrah: *Building trust with my students is important to me because I was the child of a messy divorce, and school was the only place where I felt seen.*

Sometimes people get choked up or even brought to tears by this fourth why because this is where the emotion starts to connect to your inspiration and intention.

WHY #5:
Why is Why #4 important to you?

As soon as you finish writing your answer down, you'll see that this last why is usually the watershed one. Now that you've dug super deep and pinpointed your inspiration, your intention will be right in front of you, shining like a North Star.

Phil's reply to Why #5 was: *Self-esteem is important to me because I believe confident kids turn into healthy, well-rounded adults who do good in the world.* Farrah's response was: *Being seen is important to me because I believe kids should always feel that no matter what their problems are, they are never alone.*

This last one is truly the why—the inspiration behind it all.

Phil's why: *I teach because I want kids to turn into healthy, well-rounded adults who do good in the world.*

Farrah's why: *I teach because I believe kids should always feel that no matter what their problems are, they are never alone.*

Now that you've completed the exercise, notice how you are feeling physically. Do your shoulders feel relaxed, like a weight has been lifted off them? Do you feel very buzzy and excited, like you've just had a shot of espresso? Whatever signals your body is trying to send you, sit with them for a while. If you don't feel anything, that's okay too.

Put your why up somewhere so that you'll see it every day. Although I'm not teaching music anymore, my why is still "to inspire people to discover their voice." I just do it in a different way now. Having that close by gives me a laser focus as to what's important and what's not as I set my priorities and make decisions throughout the day.

YOU DIDN'T BECOME A TEACHER TO WRITE EMAILS

The Why × 5 exercise was a big hit with the teachers, and not just Farrah and Phil. In fact, right before we went on a lunch break, Marcella, another member of the workshop group, finally opened up, too.

A little over a month ago, Marcella had just returned to her first-grade class after being on maternity leave with her first child. She described herself as often bending over backward in order to accomplish all her teaching duties. But with this huge life change, she had been really nervous about going back to work as an exhausted mom to a newborn.

When she came back to school, Marcella had been so happy to see her students. They were also excited to see her and quite interested in her baby, Veda. They'd asked her all sorts of funny questions, like: *Can she walk yet? When are you taking us to your house so we can meet her? Do you really have to wipe her butt?*

But the instant she opened her work email, her pulse started racing. Marcella was drowning in messages filled with questions that carried a lot more weight. School administrators were asking her to complete assessments that the substitute covering her leave wasn't able to get to. Colleagues were asking her to join several committees she knew she would barely have time for. Well-meaning yet somewhat pushy parents had a lot of questions about their kid's behavior and concerns about literacy milestones. Every time she made a little headway, more messages poured in.

Before Veda was born, Marcella would spend hours at home responding to parent emails and internal communications. She would always make sure each message was unique, detailed, and thoughtful. Now, though, Marcella didn't have nearly the same bandwidth. By the time she got the baby settled down for the night at 7:30 p.m., Marcella would crawl into bed herself, because in just a couple of hours she'd be up again. Then rinse and repeat. All . . . night . . . long.

Still, Marcella was trying to hold herself to the same standard. For the last couple of weeks, she'd been using her breastfeeding time to write email replies on her phone. She managed to get most of them done, but her worry about getting it all done was disrupting her sleep just as much as feeding Veda. She was a zombie at school most days, and when she got home, she was feeling tapped out and anxious instead of enjoying bonding with her baby.

Marcella admitted that she just couldn't see a path forward to *doing something* that reflected her mission because she didn't have the same capacity anymore. It wasn't only about keeping up with emails, either. She just wasn't able to stretch herself thin and juggle all her teaching responsibilities as she had done before. She was almost in tears, on the verge of giving up and quitting.

Then I asked her a simple question that left her a little taken aback: "Did you become a teacher so you could write emails?"

Marcella stood there quietly for a minute before replying, "No."

Then I asked her if she felt comfortable reading her statement of intention, and she did.

"I teach because I want my students to learn that the world is not black-and-white. There's beauty in the gray."

It was such a heartfelt sentiment that I almost choked up.

From the thoughtful look on Marcella's face, I could see that she was beginning to put the pieces together. Teachers like her, Phil, and Farrah are coming to school frustrated and worn down every day—not just because their mission isn't in plain sight, but because they're also devoting way too much of themselves to tasks that are not connected to their why.

In Marcella's case, on top of all her classroom duties, she was spending *so* much time making sure her inbox was always at zero, each person who emailed her was replied to within twenty-four hours, and every message she sent was perfectly written. She was killing herself in the process—but why? Her mission is to show her students that the world is not black-and-white, and there's beauty in the gray. Obsessing over emails is not going to support or serve her in that goal. It's only going to steal her energy and her joy.

So here's another key to changing this dynamic and showing up to your job full of passion instead of running on fumes.

Give your best effort and full attention to the tasks and practices that truly align with your mission.

Prioritize the things that help you teach with intention.

Maximize your impact by reserving your energy for whatever is going to serve you in the classroom.

I know you already have systems in place that help you make it through the workday relatively unscathed. I know you have multiple routines at work that keep your head above water. You may have even taken some shortcuts and extreme measures, just as Marcella has, to stay on top of everything that's required of you as an educator, all the while telling yourself, *It is what it is!*

I'm also not suggesting that you ditch the responsibilities that don't align, either. We all have certain obligations in our roles as educators that we're not able to dismiss. This is about approaching them and doing them differently.

Each decision you make about where you put your time and attention, you should ask yourself: Does this align with my mission/intention? Yes or no?

If it's a no, well then, it's not a top priority. The effort you put into this task cannot be 100 percent. For Marcella, that meant giving herself a more reasonable timeline to respond to emails and spending much less time drafting her replies.

And if it's a full-bodied yes, then you get to divert much more of your energy in this direction. This might seem like a small adjustment in behavior, but it's truly a game changer. When you make your mission a priority as an educator, then you don't sweat the stuff that's not supporting your intention and goals. You pour your heart and soul into the things that matter most and fill you up, while doing just enough to get the other things off your plate.

To help you make those distinctions, try this next exercise.

Exercise: Live With It, Manage It, End It

This is a variation of a task management strategy that's popular in the tech world, but it works nicely for our purposes, too, because it's based on a pretty universal principle: Not all stressors are created equal. Some stressors are just part of life, some you can manage, and some you can actually end. This exercise is all about sorting these stress-inducing things into these three categories and getting curious in the process. You might find that some things you thought you had to live with can actually be managed. And those overwhelming stressors? You might realize you can choose to stop dealing with them altogether. Basically, this is about finding your agency again.

Grab your list of stressors from chapter 1, as well as a pen or pencil and a fresh piece of paper (or print the PDF from *empowerededucator.com/book*). Start by drawing three columns, and label them *Live With It, Manage It, End It.*

Now look at your list of stressors and start to think about

which of these you simply have to live with. Take faculty meetings, for example. Whether you're leading them or just attending, they generally might not be something you look forward to with a smile on your face, right? But here's the thing: You can align these unavoidable tasks—like faculty meetings—with your personal mission. Think about how you want to show up in these situations. Do you want to be grumpy and resentful, or do you want to focus on connecting with your colleagues? What feels more aligned?

By keeping your inspiration and intention front and center, you can turn these experiences into opportunities to be the person you truly want to be . . . even though it might have felt stressful in the past. Knowing your mission gives you direction. If joy, ease, or happiness is part of your intention, think about how you want to approach those stressors with 10 percent more of that feeling. What would change? How would you shift your behavior? When you find alignment on *your* terms for those can't-avoid-them tasks and situations, everything starts to shift. Take those live-with-it stressors and write them in the first column.

Next, let's look at the stressors you can *manage*. This might mean developing a different cadence of communication or planning regular check-ins so things don't fall through the cracks. Or it might mean delegating to someone else. Yes, the task needs to get done, but does it need to be *you* who does it? (This is a great place to look at stressors in your home and personal life. Is it time, say, to get the kids packing their own lunches and doing their own laundry? Maybe!) Write those in the middle column.

And finally, decide which stressors you can end. If a fellow teacher stresses you out, makes you anxious, or just sets you on edge, you can choose not to engage with them (we'll talk about boundaries in chapter 8). If all the social interaction of the school day really drains your social battery, you can decide to eat lunch in your classroom instead of in the faculty room for a little break. These will go in that third column.

Ultimately, you may find that some of your stressors move into different categories as your life shifts—that's normal. What's important here is remembering that *you* are the variable, you're 100 percent responsible for how you show up in every space, and this kind of shift is what makes everything else you do more effective.

MAIN TAKEAWAYS

- Living your mission—or your why—as an educator helps keep you grounded and energized while increasing your impact on your students.
- You can live your mission by understanding what your inspiration is, teaching with intention, and prioritizing what aligns with your why.
- Your inspiration is what moves you to do what you do. When you get back in touch with your inspiration (through thought experiments like the Teaching Origin Story), you're able to move toward the kinds of empowering emotions that spurred you into action when you first chose this path for yourself, and rekindle the fire that fuels your work as a teacher.
- Your intentions are the promise you make to yourself to carry out your mission. Teaching with intention, not to expectations, helps you keep your promise to yourself and move through your day with

agency (an empowering emotion), rather than resignation and defeat (disempowering ones).

- Prioritizing what aligns with your mission (and understanding what you can live with, manage, or end entirely) reduces stress, gives you more time to devote to the things that matter most to you, and helps you show up with passion and enthusiasm.

3

DESIGN THE LIFE YOU'VE ALWAYS WANTED

A fellow teacher was sitting in her car in the school's parking lot before the start of the day, wondering what was going to happen during a meeting with the principal later that afternoon. The email she'd received in the morning was something along the lines of *Stop by my office before the end of the day.* Her thoughts were spiraling. *I must have said something stupid last time I was in her office. Does this mean I'm going to get fired? If I get fired, I'm not going to have any money, and then I'm going to lose my house and be homeless.*

Even though she was completely safe in the driver's seat of her Honda Accord, her nervous system was reacting as though she was actually *in* that scenario with the principal. Her pulse was racing, she was sweating like she'd just sprinted down the street, and her mouth was so parched she could down her whole raspberry iced tea in one gulp. Nothing was actually happening to her at that moment, and yet the anxious thoughts in her head had cortisol and adrenaline coursing through her bloodstream as though there was a clear and present danger to contend with.

Here's why: Her nervous system—and yours—doesn't know the difference between thoughts and what's actually happening.[1]

Fortunately, this neurobiological phenomenon (say that ten times fast!) is actually something you can leverage in your favor. By shifting your thought patterns, you can ease your body into a rest-and-repair state that allows you to feel calmer and more centered. Visualization techniques are one of the keys to flipping that switch, and you can use them for a lot of reasons. You encounter a lot of stress on the job (tricky conversations, competing demands, time crunches . . .), and visualization can help you stay grounded and reduce tension by helping you experience the feelings you want to feel in those highly charged situations.

But there's an even bigger benefit. When you visualize a unique holistic future using the same techniques, you can actually design the life you want for yourself and build it brick by brick. In other words, you can live your life by design or by default.

In a work environment that often turns chaotic, many teachers are living with their default settings on, doing what needs to be done and then moving on to the next thing without giving much thought to what they want most out of life. It's so easy to get distracted and become detached from your aspirations and hopes when your decisions are based on what you think you're supposed to do or what others believe you should do. That's why making a conscious effort to look ahead and imagine another version of yourself—one that you alone mold and shape—is just as important as having your mission on lock.

Since your mission is essentially your *why*, your vision is your *where*. In order to have a clear sense of direction, you have to understand what your destination is. Think about it: When you're using GPS to get from one place to another, you don't just enter *downtown* or *the store* into the search bar. You type a specific location into your phone so a course can be charted for you.

You get to look at your life in the same way. When you specifically picture where you want to be some five, ten, or twenty years from now, you draw a mental map that leads you out of default mode and toward a state of being that is entirely created *by* you, *for* you. Once you have the map set in your mind, it's really clear what choices will keep you on track. Cutting the BS and doing only what supports your vision and mission gets so much easier, too.

The vision you have of your future gets to be more than a series of accomplishments or milestones, like writing and publishing a book, gaining tenure, and retiring in Fiji. If you want to design your life on a solid foundation, you'll also need to consider the person you want to become, the lessons you want to learn, and most important, the emotions you want to feel along the way.

So let's dive in. This chapter is full of effective visualization experiments that are going to help you create your unique vision, some lessons in neuroscience to help change the way you think (and by extension, the way you feel about life), and an encouraging pep rally for your mind that you can revisit whenever disempowering thoughts and self-doubt try to creep in, both in and out of school.

THE VARIABLE IS YOU

You get a flat tire on the way to school. A student talks back to you in front of the whole class. A colleague criticizes your outfit and says you're dressed unprofessionally. You're late getting home to your own kids because you were cornered at the end of the day by your principal and couldn't leave work on time. Your whole evening routine is now a mess and you have no energy left to grade the stack of homework your students turned in almost a week ago.

Whether you consider that a horrible day or just a walk in the park compared to what you normally deal with, there is one universal truth that I'm sure we can all agree on: Almost everything in life is completely out of your control. Every day is filled with the unexpected and unplanned. No matter how well prepared or intuitive you might be, you can't avoid most of what the world—including the educational system—throws at you. Life gets *lifey*!

However, you *can* control your thoughts and your responses to every situation you're in.

The idea that you actually *have a say in what your brain thinks* might seem farfetched. Studies have shown that the average person thinks thousands of thoughts a day.[2] There's no way you could wrangle and redirect every single one that pops into your head!

And that's true—to an extent. Your brain synapses are firing all the time, sending messages to your body to react to your environment, mostly subconsciously. You can't intercept each and every one of them and bend them to your will. Moreover, thoughts are not facts; they are options, and not everything you think is true. But as you learned in chapter 2, you can learn to be more aware of how your thoughts inform your feelings and decisions and thus can make more conscious decisions (choosing to live by design versus by default, or with intention versus on autopilot).

Consider the teacher from above, sitting in her car, freaking out about her upcoming meeting with the principal. All her assumptions about what might happen were negative. Her thoughts were focused only on how she could have screwed up and made a mistake. She was convinced the conversation with her administrator was going to be horrible. In the next section, we'll learn more about the physiological reasons why her nervous system went into overdrive because of these thoughts, but for now, I want to point out that she has the ability to Stop and Notice. This will bring her back into her body instead of being in her head with her spinning thoughts.

She also has the power to recognize her thoughts as disempowering and decide to think a different, more empowering thought. She could tell herself that whatever the principal has to talk with her about might not have anything to do with her performance. She could tell herself that she wants her opinion on something urgent. Or she could imagine their interaction being sort of tense, but her handling it with finesse, poise, and grace. If she did all the above, she'd be more than likely to stroll into her office feeling comfortable and self-assured rather than nervous and wanting to throw up in her trash can. Our brains are wired to see the negative (more about this in chapter 4), but since thoughts are options, she'd have the opportunity to consider, *What if it all works out?*

For many of us, switching from disempowering to empowering thoughts isn't something we would want to do (or can do) with the snap of a finger. About fifty years ago, a renowned psychologist named Albert Ellis developed a framework called Rational Emotive Behavior Therapy, which is the basis for much of the cognitive therapy practices used today. His well-researched theory maintains that your thoughts are intrinsically tied to the long-held beliefs you have about yourself.[3] So if deep down you believe that you're undeserving, unlucky, or unlovable, your thoughts and actions are going to reflect that—until you choose to change that belief.

Let's say it's the middle of a school day and you're surrounded by a roomful of third graders. Your students are all at their desks, working busily under the lights, and staying cool with the air conditioning. There's a sudden power outage. Now the lights have gone out and the AC is down. Everyone is becoming hot and uncomfortable, no one can really see what they're doing, and chaos is about to break out.

If you believe that you are an awful teacher who never gets a break and has the *worst* luck, you might think to yourself, *This is a total nightmare! My lesson plan is ruined. I have to fix this or my kids are going to run riot.* After thinking those thoughts, you might proceed to run around the classroom in a panic, looking for a flashlight and battery-operated fans while ordering your students to stay quiet until you get things back on track.

But if you believe that you are the kind of person who can turn an unexpected glitch into an opportunity to have fun, your thoughts might go something like this: *This is a class of great kids. They love trying new things. I bet we can still do something in class to make good use of the time.* Then you might challenge the kids to get creative and brainstorm how they can still learn the topic without electricity. You might decide it's time to shake it up and play a good old-fashioned classroom game. Or you might declare, "You know what? Let's have class outside," and relocate everyone out to where there's sunlight and fresh air.

What does all of this have to do with your vision?

In order to live the life you design, think the way you want to think, and feel the way you want to feel, you have to take total responsibility for your thoughts, beliefs, and actions. A strong and powerful vision comes from the belief that you set the tone in any space you enter. It depends on your realizing that you're the variable in every challenging (or not-so-challenging) moment you experience. It requires you to acknowledge that you always have choices, even when it may seem like you don't.

That might feel like a lot. You are responsible for so much in every area of your life, especially in your job as a teacher. There's already so much on your plate, and it can feel easier to point a finger outward instead of taking action yourself. But that externalization leads to always being a victim of your circumstances . . . and ultimately getting more piled right back on that plate. This is about designing your own plate: making it bigger, deciding what's on it, and choosing how much of it gets your full attention. My hope is that by the end of this chapter, you'll see how shifting your beliefs and taking ownership of your life is the biggest gift you can give yourself and your students. Instead of putting the responsibility on everyone else to give you what you want, you'll view this as an opportunity to look within and access your inner power.

What if you gave yourself permission to believe in your heart that you are deserving of a life filled with whatever brings you joy and happiness? What would change?

What if you gave yourself permission to know in your bones how capable you are of changing how you think, feel, and act?

And what if you gave yourself permission to imagine your most audacious and brilliant vision of the future? Because once you catch a glimpse, you'll never let it go.

BELIEVING IS SEEING

After years of competitive swimming, Diana Nyad set out to do something that most people, even most professional athletes, would never dream of: swimming from Cuba to Florida, without a shark cage, dive fins, or rest breaks.

It didn't matter that she had already failed four times. It didn't matter that the 110-mile stretch of ocean was filled with jellyfish, unpredictable currents, and (yes) sharks. It didn't matter that she was in her sixties and the only other woman to have made the swim had been a full four decades younger (and *had* used a shark cage for protection). Whatever the obstacles in front of her, Diana knew this swim was something she would accomplish, because she'd already seen herself doing it: As she later reflected, "the vision of that crossing literally entered my imagination at the age of nine. . . . My mom pointed out across the sea and said to me: 'There. Havana is right out there. It's so close that you, you little swimmer, you could actually swim there.'"[4]

For months leading up to her fifth attempt, Diana didn't just train in the pool. She visualized the swim. She visualized herself touching the Florida shore, victorious. She visualized cutting through the dark water with her strokes, fighting off fatigue, and pushing through the pain—every moment of the swim, in vivid detail, down to the smell of the ocean around her and the sounds of the crowd cheering on the beach.

When Diana finally slipped into the Cuban waters at age sixty-four, her mind was as prepared as her body. She had already "completed" this swim hundreds of times in her visualization practice. She swam through salt abrasions and rough seas and unthinkable fatigue, and swam *toward* the vision she'd cultivated for so long: touching down on the beach. And then, after fifty-three grueling hours in the water, she emerged from the waves in Florida—the first person to complete the legendary swim without a shark cage, fins, or a break to rest.

Guess what?

You have more in common with this extraordinary swimmer than you think.

While Diana Nyad is a once-in-a-generation athlete, she

has a brain that works just like yours—and you can take advantage of how it works, just like she did.

Your brain has a high level of neuroplasticity, meaning it can grow and change throughout your lifetime. New experiences and memories, sensory stimulation and learning tasks, and a host of other factors create neural pathways and establish patterns that develop into habits and routines that your brain organizes and autosaves. Visualization taps into the same neural pathways and activates many of the same regions of your brain where real-world experiences are stored. That's one of the reasons why your brain can't always distinguish between your thoughts and actual events.

Here's how this could work during a school day. Maybe you have an important presentation coming up at parents night. You can create a vision of success, where you totally nail your speech while navigating the slideshow effortlessly. You can also visualize things not going according to plan, like technical issues, and imagine what you might do if they occur. When it comes time for you to swing into action, your brain is bound to react like it's already done this presentation multiple times and you'll feel prepared to handle whatever is out of your control.

Or maybe testing week is coming up. You can use the days leading up to the tests envisioning how stressful it's going to be, how you'll be running around without enough time, how your kids will be fidgety and not sit still, how (of *course*) the announcement for a fire drill will come over the loudspeaker and throw everything off . . . or you can visualize the testing going smoothly, calmly, and without interruption, catastrophe, or pressure from administration.

You can use the same brain hacking techniques to create your personal vision, too. Regularly picturing your *where*, including who you want to be once you get there, follows the exact same principles. The more you think about your greatest desires and ambitions and see the details of a future where you are living your very best life, the more your brain will accept those images as fact, not fiction. This doesn't mean you can just sit back and expect everything to happen for you—you still need to take action. But when your brain is fully aligned with your vision, you create a real intention behind your action. *That's* what creates embodied change. And to get your brain aligned, you need to believe that what you see is already waiting for you—and know that you deserve it.

Just like Diana Nyad's vision was there all along, even when the waters were churning around her.

VISUALIZATION IN THE CLASSROOM

While this book is focused on teachers, your students have brains, too! Imagine what would happen if you took time with your students as they visualized their graduation? Their completion of a project? Their performance of a piece of music or their feelings after they've successfully completed a test? The technique is beautifully flexible and adaptable for everyone—so go ahead and try it out.

Let's take a moment to see what's ahead for you with the following visualization exercise. This might feel new to you, because teachers aren't often asked what they want or invited to engage in a conversation about their dreams for the future—as if we're expected to just take what we get. Also, if your beliefs about yourself and what's possible get in the way a bit or if you just aren't sure you believe any of this can really work for you, that's normal. I encourage you to go into this with an open mind, like a science experiment. What would happen if you got curious about it?

For now, simply be open to whatever ideas pop into your mind and let them flock to you like birds landing on the branch of a tall, leafy tree. No judgment—you're just collecting information.

Thought Experiment: The Miracle Question

Although this is a thought experiment, it's also a really good one to write down—either in a notebook or on the worksheet at *empowerededucator.com/book*.

Imagine you went to bed one night, and when you woke up the next morning, by some miracle, everything you wanted already existed. What would you notice right away? How would you know things have changed? What can you observe?

Imagine what your day would be like in this new reality of yours. How do you feel when you wake up? How do you experience your morning? Where would you go, and how are you showing up in these spaces? Maybe you're doing something you really enjoy and can be fully present for all of it instead of worrying about work. What would your interactions with people be like? What's it like going into the school building?

Now the million-dollar question: How do you feel—emotionally and physically—now that you got your miracle? Would you walk around with a smile plastered on your face because you're so damn happy? Would your tension headaches be gone? Would you kick your feet up and stretch out on the couch, feeling completely content and relaxed? Would your insomnia go away? Would you walk into any room totally confident and energized?

Now bring your attention to how you feel right now in

your current reality. You'll most likely notice a gap between where you are and where you would be if your miracle happened.

The key here is that you've revealed something very important: a holistic vision for your life that you can start creating for yourself today—no miracle required.

DECLARING IS PLANNING

When it comes to your vision, declarations wield power and agency. They are the building-block ideas that create your overall design. Like the outline of a novel before it's written, a sketch of a portrait before it's painted, or a blueprint of a home before it's constructed, declarations are pieces of a grand plan that is being put into motion.

But the plan can work only if your ideas are concrete, specific, and based on what you *do* want—not what you *don't* want. Your brain is wired to focus on what you're telling it to pay attention to, so if you're only declaring what you *don't* want, your mind will capture only the things you're telling yourself not to see.

For instance, if someone says to you, "Don't think of a blue elephant," what's the first thing that automatically comes to mind?

Yep, a blue elephant.

When you declare what you *do* want and are incredibly specific, then your brain becomes hyperfocused on that. Just like Diana Nyad visualizing her successful swim, you can use your thoughts to create outcomes and assess all the ways you might possibly accomplish them. You begin plotting your next move toward your *where*. Declaring becomes an activating agent, kind of like the yeast that gets the bread dough to rise.

Simply put, you move closer to the vision you want.

If you're feeling stuck, try listing what you *don't* want and then write the opposite as a start to your vision. What's most important is that you keep your eyes and mind open to other possibilities. When you allow your thoughts to be boundless and drift toward things that bring you closer to how you want to feel, eventually your vision is going to become clearer and more precise. The more pressure you put on yourself, the more you'll lock yourself into your current pattern and environment. So give yourself grace and room to see whatever comes into view without any judgment. Be curious and adventurous.

Exercise: A Letter from Your Future Self

This letter-writing exercise is one of my favorite visualization experiments to do both with the teachers I work with and by myself. In fact, I do this very exercise once every year as I create my own vision.

Even though most of the "letters" we write nowadays are emails, I recommend doing this old-school and writing it out by hand on paper—handwriting forces you to slow down, get more intentional, and do so without digital distractions (like open tabs).

Start off by dating this letter a year from now. Since this experiment is about being very specific with your vision, it's important to keep your thoughts in the relatively near future, knowing and believing that whatever is on the horizon already exists.

Next, address the letter to yourself. It's a gentle reminder that the power of changing your life is in your own hands!

Now, picture all the amazing things that you want to

happen in the upcoming year. They get to be the big and bold dreams that align with everything you laid out in the Miracle Question thought experiment. Maybe you hope to start the book you've always wanted to write or to be interviewed by a local newspaper or TV station about a school event you're leading. Maybe you want to buy some land and build a house, or exercise regularly and actually run that marathon. Maybe you want to be more present with your family (and maybe set some boundaries with your mother-in-law). Everything is available to you. You can reach for whatever feels aligned and right to you. Most important, write about how you've *felt* this past year: *I go through my day feeling a sense of ease*; *I laugh a lot; I am present with my kids and feel so much joy;* or whatever resonates for you.

As a disclaimer here, if the answer to your Miracle Question was "win the lottery and retire early to Fiji," that all sounds great, but more important, consider what feelings are underneath that desire. *That's* the stuff that you get to focus on in your vision that will lead you to what you want.

Notice how good you're feeling as you think these thoughts. Call on that positive energy as fuel while you write all these desires down in your letter. Use the past tense to tell yourself everything that you've done.

Remember, your brain believes what it sees. By creating this image as if you've already done these things, you're much more likely to start to believe it is all possible. Writing in the past tense also helps create a sense of safety in our brains—we'll get into why that matters in the next chapter, but for now, just know that your brain inherently goes to negative places when faced with something new. So thinking about a significant life change before it actually occurs can give your brain a chance to become more familiar and relaxed about it.

Once you're finished with your letter, read it back to yourself. Note that this isn't an invitation to doubt what you've written and adjust it. This is about declaring to yourself: *This is my vision. This is what I want and who I am one year from now.*

It's simple yet powerful. The teachers I've done this exercise with have gone on to (in no particular order): spend Sundays playing games with their kids instead of worrying about the week ahead; finally book that dream vacation to Ireland; lose sixty pounds; and even discover one evening that she was cooking dinner with her son—something that she had written down in her vision almost a year prior and forgotten about until it came true!

In fact, at one time, this book that you're reading now existed only in my imagination. While it took much longer than a year, I consistently visualized how I'd feel writing this book and what impact it would have. This vision kept me crystal clear on *where* I was heading and informed my actions along the way. It was more than a goal. Goals can be great, but they often focus on nothing but the external. Visualization encompasses both the external and the internal by incorporating how you want to feel at every step.

The last thing you need to do is find an easily accessible place to store this letter. Whenever you're feeling a little adrift, like you're losing sight of what your vision is, pull out this letter and read it to yourself until you can visualize everything in it clearly enough that you can touch it. Pay attention to how you are feeling as you do this—grounded, fired up, at peace, etc.—and know that you can carry that feeling with you now because everything is already in motion.

You have just declared it so.

YOU RECEIVE WHAT YOU BELIEVE YOU DESERVE

Now that you have designed a vision, it can be paired with your mission, and together they will guide you throughout your life and your work as an educator. Like guardrails on a winding road, they can help you make decisions that fully align with your *why* and your *where* instead of taking you off course or keeping you stuck.

Once you've made a declaration, you're that much more open to see possibilities that align with what you want.

If you're a new teacher and part of your vision is to have a large group of work friends that you're close with until you retire, accept that invitation to your colleague's networking happy hour or monthly book club (or start one yourself). If a piece of your vision is to be totally debt-free and pay for your child's college education, then enroll in the free financial literacy program at your local library or download a bunch of e-books on the subject from their online collection.

The big trick here, though, is to make choices that support your vision. If you want to receive what you declare, your choices must reflect the vision you believe in *and* the belief that you're deserving of your vision being fulfilled. As teachers, you make countless compromises to get through each day—sometimes because it's the best way forward in the moment, and because martyrdom has become culturally ingrained in our profession.

But when it comes to your vision, there is no halfway. No gray area.

Either you decide to honor yourself or you choose to betray yourself. Either you move the needle forward or you don't.

Let's go back to that hypothetical teacher, freaking out in her car before her big meeting. The good news is, she managed to pull herself together before that emergency meeting with her principal. First she did a few rounds of cleansing breaths. Then she visualized conversations with the principal that were in line with her vision. She knew that while she enjoyed being an educator, when she saw herself in the future, she was principal. She'd already started on her administrative certification. She knew she was a great problem solver and communicator. She had a lot of ideas on how to lead.

So the first thing she visualized was sitting down with her principal in her office and noticing how she felt. She wasn't feeling intimidated, anxious, or timid anymore. She felt calm, grounded, and confident, as if she was talking to a peer, one whom she respected and trusted, with the full knowledge that she was just as capable as her supervisor. She *felt* as though she was the sort of person who could be—who would be—a principal, too.

Soon she was feeling so much better, her pulse began returning to normal. Yes, she had no idea what her principal's intentions were for this meeting. But as she walked into the building, she did so with confidence, as if she deserved for her vision to come true, simply because she wanted it to.

When she went into the office, the principal got to the point right away. There was an opportunity to have a student teacher in some classrooms next semester. Would she want her classroom to be one of these?

Because she was already working on her certification, she didn't have the time to manage a student teacher, so she politely declined. She could have agreed, because it might have made her less uncomfortable to just say yes. But if she had, she would be veering off the road instead of staying within the guardrails. She knew she deserved to receive what she declared, so she decided to honor herself. Instead, she chose the discomfort of staying true to her vision instead of the discomfort of her default setting of *Do what others ask, because teachers put everyone else first.* (Notice: There's a sense of discomfort either way. But I promise you, the discomfort of growth is always more exciting and expansive than the discomfort of staying the same.)

As a former classroom teacher, I understand that sometimes saying no is a tough ask because there are so many people counting on you, especially your students. But how do you want to show up? What message do you want to send to your students? Do you want them to see self-sacrifice as the only way to "be good" in life?

Or do you want them to understand that everyone has a true vision for themselves that they need to honor—and that they get to make choices accordingly?

If it's the latter, then remember to tell yourself this:

I deserve to feel joy.

I am worthy of the vision I've designed.

I have one life to live, and it can be whatever I want it to be.

This is how I get to make the most impact.

MAIN TAKEAWAYS

- ✦ You are the variable in every situation you encounter. While you can't control what happens to you, you can control your thoughts and responses.
- ✦ Your brain doesn't always distinguish between your thoughts and reality, which means you can use

visualization techniques to create neural pathways that support the life you want to design.

- A strong vision requires you to be specific about what you want, not about what you don't want. Your brain focuses on whatever you direct its attention toward.

- Declaring your vision makes it tangible and real. When you put a stake in the ground about your future, you activate your brain to start moving toward that reality.

- You must believe you deserve to receive what you declare. Half-hearted commitment to your vision will keep you stuck in default mode instead of moving toward your desired life.

- Living your vision means making choices that align with your *where*, even when those choices feel uncomfortable or go against the expectations of others. It's not about passively waiting for your vision to come true, but actively pursuing it with your brain fully on board.

4

REWIRE YOUR BRAIN

I was a confident, newly certified teacher when I met Jeremiah, a sweet but completely unmotivated student in my seventh-grade general music class. Jeremiah played the guitar and was quite talented for a twelve-year-old. He had a natural ability but not enough drive to practice at home or try his best when he was in class.

Honestly, most of my students were just like Jeremiah—somewhat interested in their instrument, but too distracted by puberty to really care. Nothing made me feel more out of my depth than teaching this class. Educators are supposed to be lighting fires under their students, but I couldn't seem to do that with them, especially Jeremiah. On a good day, when I listened to him play, I could see him on a stage somewhere, playing to an energized crowd of fans. But on a bad day, he was irritable and refused to even participate.

I felt confident teaching these kids, but I wasn't getting the response I'd expected. Fresh out of college, I knew my content like the back of my hand, had a solid understanding of the pedagogy required, and even got an A on my paper on my philosophy of music education. What the hell was going on? Why did I feel so unprepared?

But then something clicked, and it occurred to me what was missing. I realized that I didn't fully understand my students as adolescents, particularly where they were at this stage in their brain development. So I thought maybe learning more about how their adolescent minds worked would help me be a better communicator and connect with them on a deeper level.

Once I got curious about this, I spent hours after school deep in cognitive development and neuroscience research (I was living my best nerd life!). As I'd hoped, everything I learned about the human brain changed my approach to teaching and strengthened my ability to engage my students. For example, once I knew autonomy was especially important during this stage of development, I made sure to include opportunities for personal choices in every lesson. Since I understood that my students were going through profound physical changes, their fidgetiness in class became less of a distraction because I used movement every chance I could.

What surprised me the most, however, was how much this newfound knowledge transformed the way I lived my life. I went from believing that our brains controlled everything about us to realizing that we can in fact direct our brains to behave and act in any way we want. You can navigate what your brain is doing based on its need to survive, and when we know the right techniques and methods to help us work *with* our neurobiology, we're capable of anything.

This ability—*metacognition*—is fundamental to everything I do. The term comes from the Greek word *meta,* meaning "above," and the Latin word *cognitio,* meaning "thinking" or "knowledge," and it refers to, basically, *thinking about think-*

ing. In other words, it's just the act of becoming more aware of our thought processes.

A practice of metacognition is something I like to refer to as "thought scanning"—the same way bags get scanned at airport security, *you* can scan your thoughts. Think of how the conveyor belt slowly brings suitcases, bags, and backpacks through the X-ray machine one at a time so that the agents can inspect what's inside and be sure to handle anything that looks suspect. Now imagine that you can slow down your thinking, scan each piece of thought-baggage as it passes through your mind, and decide—based on what you observe—what you want to do with it.

Metacognition matters because it empowers us. As you'll learn in this chapter, our brains are hardwired to protect us from harm and keep us safe while simultaneously juggling a million other tasks. Our brain is so efficient that we often walk around on autopilot yet never wander outside our comfort zone. Thought scanning is the great disrupter. It wakes us up to what's possible if we learn how to observe and interpret our thoughts—from an objective point of view. Once we hone this skill, we have an essential tool that will help us create change and guide us closer to our vision.

Through thought scanning, you become more in tune with what brings you happiness and then make choices that align with your joy. You're more aware of why you've made unwise decisions and begin to break unhealthy patterns. You notice what drains your energy and shift your focus toward things that make you feel vibrant and alive. Nothing is off the table, honestly. That's how powerful you are!

In this chapter, we'll cover the brain basics (like what your amygdala and prefrontal cortex do, how neural pathways are formed, and how it all got to work like that) and dig into the scientific evidence for how powerful thought scanning can be.

Finally, I'll walk you through the metacognition strategies you can use to become a highly aware thinker, a happier person, and a better teacher.

YOU ARE NOT YOUR BRAIN

I was at one of my favorite restaurants in Ithaca, New York, having brunch with Sarah, a friend who teaches fourth grade. Just as we were syruping our stack of silver dollar pancakes, the conversation took a turn when she started venting about another teacher in her building.

"I swear, every time I walk past Rose's classroom, her students are quietly working together, they're well-behaved, and her bulletin boards always look amazing," Sarah said, stabbing at her pancakes with more force than necessary. "I feel like my lessons often fall flat, a handful of my kids refuse to do any work, and I don't have the time to spend on making Pinterest-worthy bulletin boards." She paused, and then her voice got quieter, almost ashamed. "What am I missing? Maybe I'm not cut out for this the way other teachers are. I feel like I'm a bad teacher."

"Not at all." I looked her right in the eye. "These are just thoughts, and you are not your thoughts. You are not your brain."

The truth is, these feelings are far more common in our profession than we'd like to admit. Teaching can feel isolating, and when we see colleagues seemingly thriving while we struggle, it's natural—though uncomfortable—to feel that twinge of comparison. As a result, we might catch ourselves—as Sarah did—thinking less than charitable thoughts about ourselves because of the emotions stirring up in our brain.

However, given the work you've been doing over the last three chapters, maybe you see where I am going with this.

Your brain has many different important functions, but as I've mentioned before, its main job is to keep you safe and away from harm. In Sarah's case, Rose's classroom felt like a threat to Sarah's *own* relationship with her class. The intense physical response, the overwhelming feelings it stirred up, the antagonistic thoughts it triggered . . . none of that was Sarah's fault. Her brain, just like yours and mine, is wired to have that knee-jerk response when it senses a threat—even if that threat is just "another teacher doing better at something I want to succeed at." The important thing to recognize—as I reminded Sarah in the moment—is that *you are not your brain.* Remember, you have thousands of thoughts every day that are options—not facts. Could you imagine if you actually believed some of the crazy thoughts you think? Yes, your thoughts are powerful, and yes, you even have the ability to influence them. But your brain and its contents are entirely separate from who you are as a person. When you conflate the two, like Sarah was doing, it can become a mental roadblock that will get in the way of your progress and growth.

Seeing your brain as a fixed point and believing that you are indistinguishable from it make it hard to believe that change is possible. Assuming that your *brain* is in control of *you*—the decider-in-chief who dictates everything—forfeits all the agency you really and truly do have. And attaching a moral value to yourself because of your thoughts—like the way Sarah was judging herself based on the thoughts she had about herself—is the king of disempowering emotions.

Metacognition helps in interrupting these assumptions and

reclaiming your sense of agency, and that starts with the simple recognition that *you are not your brain*. You are a person who *has* a brain.

Next, you can do something we've already practiced: Stop and Notice. That's what Sarah ended up doing: Even though she'd been hard on herself for her thoughts at first, my gentle reminder that *you are not your brain* got her back on track, and she took a few deep breaths right there in the restaurant to get her nervous system regulated.

But the full power of metacognition is more than simply noticing and self-regulating. It's also about replacing those thoughts with something that feels more empowering. As a start, learning about the parts of the brain and what they do can help create an even bigger separation between your perception of who you are and what your brain is and does.

THE CURIOUS CASE OF PHINEAS GAGE

There is one person in the field of neuroscience who is absolutely legendary because of his brain: Phineas Gage.

Phineas has become the cornerstone of neuroscience education for a reason—his story is "you can't make these things up" levels of unbelievable. A railroad worker in nineteenth-century New England, Phineas was working with explosives to blast through some debris when a nearby iron rod happened to bang against a rock. Unfortunately for Phineas, the rogue spark caught the nearby gunpowder and sent the iron rod rocketing right through his eye socket. *Yikes.* (Admittedly, this story has always made me a little squeamish.)

The wildest part? Phineas survived.

Not only survived, in fact, but didn't even lose consciousness! Just a few minutes later, he was speaking, eventually was able to walk around, and even got back to work in a matter of months.

How is this possible? Because, as fate would have it, the iron rod injured only *certain parts* of Phineas's brain—and his life post-injury became a kind of inadvertent living experiment in neuroscience. Looking at what became of Phineas after his accident, we can pinpoint how the different regions of the brain work (or don't work) and how that affects our daily life as humans.

To start, Phineas was reported to have had no major memory loss as a result of his accident. Incredible, right? Maybe even . . . highly unlikely, until you realize that later medical scans revealed that his *hippocampus* was undamaged by the rod.

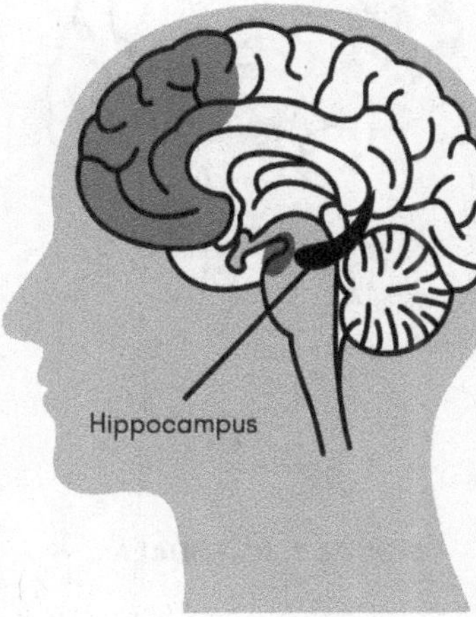

FIGURE 1: HIPPOCAMPUS

The hippocampus is the part of the brain that plays a key role in your memory (as well as in some of your emotional regulation). If you've seen the movie *Inside Out,* you can think of the hippocampus as the place where all those memory orbs are stored in Riley's brain: It forms those memories, aids in learning (because what is learning if not making and recalling memories?), and connects emotions to the memories in storage. The hippocampus is part of what's known as the limbic system of the brain: the structures in and around the cortex (or center) of the brain that process sensory input and regulate emotions. (You may have heard of the limbic system referred to as our "lizard brain," which isn't *exactly* accurate, but it is the region of the brain that deals with immediate stimuli and so-called lower-order emotions.)

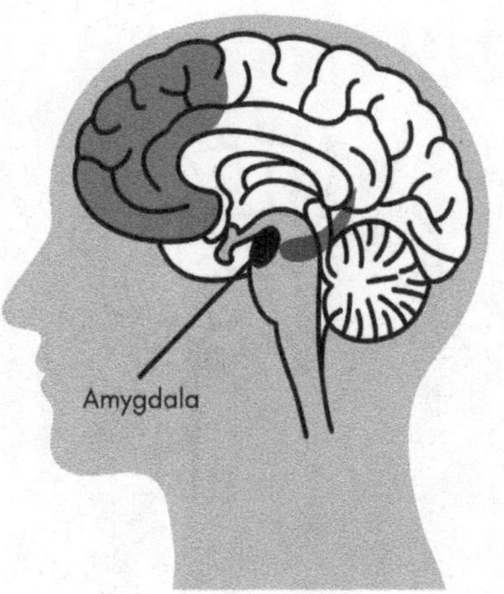

FIGURE 2: AMYGDALA

Another part of the limbic system—one also untouched by the iron rod in Phineas's head—is the *amygdala*, a teeny-tiny almond-shaped region (the word *amygdala* means "almond" in Latin) in each hemisphere of the brain responsible for behavior regulation and your stress response. When the amygdala perceives danger in some way, it puts up a big WARNING sign. Sometimes it senses danger simply from things that are new or outside your comfort zone (since your brain has no evidence of your surviving this new thing). Or it can set off the alarm bells just by recalling a memory of a highly charged past experience. These abilities play a crucial role in keeping us alive. (Like how we don't cross the road if there are cars driving past, or why we don't touch a hot stove. *Thanks, amygdala!*)

But just because his hippocampus and amygdala were safe and sound doesn't mean Phineas got off easy. While he retained the memories and motor skills necessary to maintain an independent life, he was—as his acquaintances put it—"no longer Gage." Previously a hardworking, dependable kind of fellow, Phineas was now impatient and impulsive. Where he had once been fairly mild-mannered, he was now "gross, profane, coarse, and vulgar."[1]

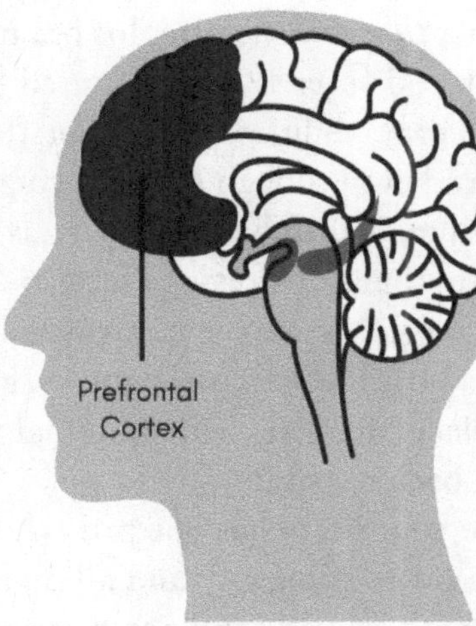

FIGURE 3: PREFRONTAL CORTEX

All of this was due to the critical region of his brain where the rod *did* do serious damage: his *prefrontal cortex*. This part of the brain—which resides in the front of your head, right above the eye sockets—is responsible for things like higher-order thinking, prioritizing, organizing, creativity, and problem-solving. It takes the input from the limbic system and interprets it: controlling impulses, weighing options, and deciding what to do when. (Incidentally, the prefrontal cortex doesn't fully develop until you're in your mid to late twenties. So if you have any "what was I thinking?" decisions from your college years—or if you're teaching teenage students—just know that part of the questionable decision-making was because that part of your brain wasn't fully cooked yet!) With his prefrontal cortex skewered, Phineas was literally unable to stop himself from swearing up a storm or flitting from one task to the next: His brain simply didn't have the capacity for it anymore. When his amygdala fired out warning signs, he didn't have the filter in place to judge which signs to act on and which ones to reevaluate.

In short, Phineas was still able to function, go about his day, and live another *twelve years* after his brain injury, but the damage of the iron rod severely compromised his *metacognitive* and *self-regulatory* abilities because of the areas of his brain it affected. And even though the metacognitive region of *your* brain is (presumably) unharmed by stray metal rods, it can still go offline in times of stress. In fact, an aggressive fear response from the amygdala can temporarily hijack your brain, causing you to act a little like Phineas: panicky, loose-cannon-y, and all-over-the-place stressed, with minimal self-regulatory abilities to get you back to baseline.

This is because your brain has one primary mission: make sure you stay alive by avoiding any and all danger. And to do that, it relies on *fear*—something your brain is really, really good at, thanks to the limbic system.

The limbic system (including the hippocampus and amygdala) hasn't evolved much since the days we were hunting and gathering and being chased by predators. In those circumstances, fear was often warranted (hungry predators are scary, after all) and the limbic system's powerful ability to spike you into *fight-or-flight mode* could get you ready to sprint for your life at a moment's notice.

The problem in modern life is that the amygdala is wired to treat anything out of the ordinary as a red-alert threat, which means even non-life-threatening situations that are unfamiliar (a difficult conversation with a colleague, a challenging text message) can prompt your amygdala to send out big DANGER! DANGER! signals. That fear response triggers all the physical symptoms we've discussed (like a racing pulse, sweating palms, a churning stomach) and also feels *exhausting* (because it takes a lot of energy to get your body that keyed up).

The kicker? When your fear response is activated, your brain also *shuts down* any "unnecessary" parts. Since you don't need to think creatively and prioritize and organize when you're being chased by a predator (or so your brain reasons), you don't actually need to be fueling that part of your brain. In response, your brain "helpfully" takes your prefrontal cortex (aka the part of the brain that Phineas lost use of in his accident) offline.

So if you've ever felt like it's physically difficult to get out of your comfort zone, *you're not wrong.* You're actually very, very right. In fact, your amygdala would rather you *never* did anything outside of your comfort zone because it knows that if you just continue to do the same things—even when the status quo is not serving your mission and vision—you are still safe and alive. Feelings of fear happen when you are outside of your comfort zone. While you might not be in any danger, your amygdala responds *as though you are* because it doesn't have any evidence that you've survived the new thing you're trying (or has a memory/knowledge of negative consequences from similar circumstances—that's the hippocampus chiming in). This can even happen when you are just *thinking* about stressors or when the new experience is something objectively safe and healthy. In fact, if you are a person who perpetually lives in pressure and worry, feeling relaxed or calm is going to set off an amygdala activation—there's no *evidence* of your just *feeling carefree on a Sunday* and *surviving*!

Thankfully, *you* are not a nineteenth-century railroad worker in the days before proper safety training, and you *do* have access to your prefrontal cortex. You can utilize this incredible part of your brain to be curious, and Nancy Drew your feelings. And by understanding the other parts of your brain that are responsible for emotional responses (like the hippocampus and amygdala) you can learn how to create safety for your nervous system by self-regulating even more effectively. That's what will help you show up as your best self and align with your mission and vision.

Exercise: More Self-Regulation Practices

The vagus nerve (named for the Latin word for "wanderer") is the longest nerve in the body: It attaches the brain stem to the body, travels down your throat to your chest, and goes all the way through your abdomen. This long-reaching pathway is responsible for regulating the physical manifestations of the state of your nervous system and plays a central part in what's called the *parasympathetic nervous system*. When the vagus nerve is engaged, your nervous system is in a rest-and-digest state and is no longer in fight-or-flight mode (the *sympathetic system*).

Polyvagal theory, as pioneered by Dr. Stephen Porges, has shown that stimulating the vagus nerve can get the parasympathetic system back online, effectively calming you down through this one mighty neural pathway.[2]

One of the quickest ways to stimulate the vagus nerve is movement. You don't have to do CrossFit or run a marathon. All it takes is small movements that you can do easily just sitting where you are.

> **TRY THIS:** Grab your elbows with your hands and shake your body back and forth, then raise your arms (still holding on to your elbows) over your head. Keep moving back and forth as you bring your arms slowly back down—and remember to breathe. Now relax your shoulders and notice again how your body feels. (If it feels nice, do it twice!)

Another great way to activate the vagus nerve is through an interesting body hack known as the *mammalian diving reflex*. As air-breathing animals, we're wired to conserve energy when we go underwater and hold our breath—which in practice means our parasympathetic nervous system comes online to slow our heart rate and calm our breathing.

> **TRY THIS:** For the full experience, fill a bowl with ice water, take a deep breath, and plunge your face in the water (yes, really!). Hold your breath for 15 to 30 seconds, then lift your face out of the water. (Try to make sure your eyes and temples are submerged to ensure you're activating the *trigeminal nerve* in that area.) Dry off and take a slow, deep breath—you'll be astounded how much calmer you feel. If you're not in a place to

dunk your head in water (i.e., at school), you can hold an ice cube or a cold pack to your temples and hold your breath for a similar calming effect.

Finally, you can promote communication between the hemispheres of your brain—and overall neural communication—by engaging in some bilateral movement like a cross crawl as made popular by Brain Gym.[3] Moving across your body's midline helps the left side of your brain talk to the right, and vice versa.

TRY THIS: While standing, tap your right hand to your right knee, then your left hand to your left knee. Next, tap your right hand to your left knee and your left hand to your right knee. Repeat this sequence three times. (Don't forget to breathe!)

Remember, your feelings happen in your body and not in your mind. Your thoughts are in your mind. So even though we may be thinking stressful thoughts, we need to do something with our stress in the body to fully process what we're feeling and let our amygdala know that we're safe. For more self-regulation resources, go to *empowerededucator.com/book*.

YOUR BRAIN'S GATEKEEPER: THE RETICULAR ACTIVATING SYSTEM

Marlon was a middle school teacher I met at an annual education convention in Texas. We were at an evening social event after a long day of workshops when Steve, a colleague we both knew, introduced us.

Well, it wasn't actually an introduction. Steve was telling me about his school year, and he mentioned that his coworker

Marlon was here with him. Then out of nowhere, a man sidled up next to Steve and said, "You rang?"

Marlon was a hoot right out of the gate.

Once Steve went off to get something to drink, Marlon and I started chatting. In just a few minutes, we found out we had a lot in common. We both grew up in New York, we were the same age, and we even had the same favorite movie.

At the same time, we *didn't* seem to feel the same way about the convention. I was invigorated, inspired, and full of excitement, while Marlon was . . . less enthusiastic.

"I hate coming to these things," Marlon said as he took a sip of his drink. "The attendees are the same every year. The panel conversations always seem to have these speakers who can't stay on point. And the topics are often boring and tired. Oh, and don't get me started on the crowds and the lines."

As I listened to Marlon's list of criticisms, I nodded silently. He was certainly entitled to his own opinion, of course. Since we were fellow teachers, he obviously felt comfortable sharing his point of view without holding anything back, and that made me smile. But later that night in my hotel room, I kept thinking about the vastly different experiences Marlon and I had had even though we were at the same event. There are a lot of reasons that could have been the case—personal preference, for one thing. Maybe I love the energy of big crowds and Marlon wasn't a fan because he found them overwhelming. Maybe Marlon was just grouchy from weak hotel coffee and a stressful travel situation and my day had gone much more smoothly.

But in the end, there was one major difference that seemed obvious: *Marlon and I were paying attention to completely different things.*

While Marlon was focused on the repetitive nature of annual conventions in general—the same attendees and familiar presentation topics—I was paying attention to the enlightening discussions I was having with other educators and the quality time we had together outside of the schools we worked at. Everywhere Marlon went, he was seeing lines of people as annoying traffic, and he was aggravated. Everywhere *I* went, I was seeing people inspired into action and moving toward what interested them, so I was thrilled.

Now, you might read this and think I'm saying it's all a matter of "looking on the bright side," or something like that, and while it might seem that way, there is in fact—*surprise!*—much more that's going on here neurologically.

Remember when I told you that Marlon sauntered over to me and Steve as soon as he heard his name? The reason why his ears picked up on that while there was so much conversation going on around us was because of the brain's reticular activating system (RAS).

The RAS serves as a kind of data information filter. You can think of it like an administrative assistant in an office fielding a bunch of requests on behalf of the CEO and making the boss aware of only the most critical things that are happening. Believe it or not, there are *millions* of stimuli in your environment at any given time. But you actually experience far, *far* fewer than that (as in, less than fifty) because the RAS tells your brain what's important to pay attention to at the moment and what isn't. The sound of your own name—like Marlon picked up on—is one of those things that the RAS will let through to the top.

Here's a quick real-world example of the RAS at work. Let's say you are thinking about buying a car and you really want a Mazda CX-5. You go to the dealership and test-drive a nice blue one. As you're driving down the highway, you think to yourself, *Yep, that Mazda really is the car that I've always wanted!* But when you return to the dealership and talk about costs with the salesperson, you decide to mull the purchase over for a week.

During that week, you see Mazda CX-5s everywhere. At the gas station. In the shopping center parking lot. At stoplights. Suddenly you're like a magnet for Mazdas! It almost seems unbelievable—like it can't be just a coincidence.

Well, on a certain level, it's not. Your RAS is acting like a magnet, pulling your attention to things you told your brain were important to you. Those Mazdas were always around; they just never made it into your line of sight because they didn't make it past your brain's filter. To put it another way, as soon as you started focusing your attention on blue Mazdas, your brain was like, "I'm on it!"

Understanding how the RAS works matters because it's directly related to the fact that you *can* influence your thoughts—a very important piece of the puzzle, in fact. If you are constantly placing your attention on things like conflict or resistance or difficulty, your reticular activating system is going to react and select stimuli that align with that focus. For example, if you go to work thinking to yourself, *I never have enough time for myself,* then your RAS will show you even more evidence of how much you have on your plate and how jam-packed your day is getting. Even if you do have a few hours of uninterrupted time to yourself here and there, you are not likely to notice because you've already told your brain that it's not important enough to be on your radar.

Let's go back to Marlon again. Before I went to the convention, I was pretty psyched. I love traveling and getting to meet new people, and my attention was focused on the things I always look forward to at these events—interacting with my peers and talking about teaching methods for hours are my jam. So when I got there, that's what my brain paid attention to. It picked up on what was important to me and then said, "You got it, girl!"

Marlon, on the other hand, was probably dreading this

convention from the start. He'd been to it a number of times and had made up his mind that he wasn't going to enjoy it much. When he arrived, his brain verified each and every thing he decided to pay attention to by selecting the information that corresponded with his thoughts.

Guess who went home feeling recharged and who went home uninspired?

That said, let's take a quick pause for clarity: Again, I'm not saying you simply need to find the silver linings to avoid any emotions that don't feel good. My point is, thanks to how your brain is wired, you're always going to find what you look for—and you can leverage that to your advantage if you're strategic about it.

For example, let's bring this all back to your vision. Imagine the version of yourself that's already living in the future you've designed. What things is that person paying attention to every day? Does Future You focus more on what serves you well or more on the things you find annoying?

When you start thinking from a different vantage point, then you're able to make changes to what you pay attention to and take the necessary steps to become the person you want to be. Instead of asking yourself, *What do I need to be paying attention to?* ask, *What does my future self pay attention to?*

FEEDBACK LOOPS AND THE SAME OLD STORIES

Imagine you have a seventh-grade student who comes to math class in a *terrible* mood. Caden—your student—didn't have anything to eat at lunch the period before because he was really nervous about a big test you're about to give. And minutes before he entered the room, his friends were teasing him about the T-shirt he was wearing (apparently the Avengers are lame now?), so now he's feeling self-conscious about that, too.

As soon as the kids log on to their laptops to take the test, Caden has a vivid memory of these same friends making fun of him for failing a math test or two last year. His parents even got him a tutor for a little while, and he was embarrassed by it. Now he's developed this belief that he's terrible at math. He just doesn't get it. What's the point of even trying?

While he's taking the test, Caden is grumpy. He keeps thinking to himself, *This is too hard. You're no good at math.*

Then midway through the test, he feels kind of defeated. Suddenly he can't sit still. He is shifting in his seat and fidgeting. He wants to get up and move around, but he's not allowed to during a test.

So now Caden's behavior changes. Instead of concentrating, his attention is drifting off. He's daydreaming. Looking out the window. He's in his own little world, imagining himself playing soccer, which is something he loves to do.

Then you tell the class they have two minutes left to complete the test. But Caden's not close to being finished. He has to rush through the rest of the questions.

Time is up.

His results are revealed. He got only 42 percent of the answers right.

Caden isn't surprised. He's never going to understand this stuff.

That evening, when he's having dinner with his parents, they ask him about the test.

Caden shrugs. "I told you. I'm not good at math," he says. Then he grabs his soccer ball and goes into the backyard to play.

This scenario illustrates how even when you are young,

your thoughts create stories about who you are and the world around you in order to make sense of your experience. It's all a part of how your brain functions.

Remember, the reticular activating system is like that magnet, pulling your attention to what you've decided is important and "true" according to your own experiences. And while there's a good neurological purpose behind it, this can impact your perception and interpretation of events. In fact, your entire brain has so much input to sift through every moment you're conscious, while simultaneously navigating all the subconscious information—how you're feeling on a particular day; a catalog of memories that can be unlocked in a split second; your beliefs about yourself, your values, and your relationships—that it relies on "known" narratives to make sense of it all. A story about your life gets written in your mind, and when there seems to be evidence to prove it's all true, that story feels like fact.

Except a lot of the time . . . it's not.

Let's go back to our student who believes that he's not good at math. This is not up for debate, folks! There is evidence that backs it up. Caden failed the test, right?

Yes. And at the same time we can objectively see that there were a lot of factors that played into the test results. Remember—two things can be true at the same time.

Caden was nervous and didn't eat anything at lunch. Just like that famous Snickers slogan, *You're not you when you're hungry!*, Your mood is affected as well as your cognitive abilities.

Caden's friends were picking on his clothes, which made him remember how they roasted him for flunking math tests last year. Naturally, his confidence was affected, which isn't a great headspace for taking tests.

Caden was also restless at his desk and distracted. Not because he's not good at math, but because of everything that had happened before he even sat down.

Sure, it's easy to connect all these dots as an outside observer, but when you're in your own head, it can be far trickier. Because of how the brain is wired to distort information or generalize from it, we're all susceptible to a psychological phenomenon known as confirmation bias (more on that in chapter 5). This happens when your subconscious mind interprets information in ways that confirm your preexisting beliefs or values while ignoring or disregarding evidence that suggests there might be another point of view or explanation.

That's exactly what you saw with Caden. The grade on his test was the only piece of information his mind needed to confirm this belief that he was terrible at math. Even though there was plenty of data to support the idea that he was actually just having a stressful day, he either couldn't or wouldn't see that another story was possible.

In order to get a different external outcome, you need to change the *internal* story first. That's how you can make the RAS work for you instead of against you. And I know from experience (and science-backed research) that the more aware you are of the thoughts that shape your story, while remembering your thoughts aren't facts, the more likely you are to be able to decide which thoughts you attach your beliefs to and which thoughts aren't serving you.

As I've mentioned before, your thoughts are powerful. Every time you attach to a thought, it turns on neurocircuitry in your brain, which produces neurochemicals that trigger a feeling in your body.[4] That feeling in your body then informs your behavior. Your behavior yields a result, which often affirms your beliefs.

It's a feedback loop that can be harmful if you're attaching your beliefs to disempowering thoughts. But it's one that can also be leveraged for good, if you attach your beliefs to *empowering* thoughts instead—and to do that, you can choose to exercise *discernment*.

Discernment is how you can change those disempowering thoughts because it allows you to step back and evaluate whether a thought is actually moving you toward who you want to be. Instead of automatically believing every thought that pops into your head, discernment gives you the power to pause and ask: "Is this thought helping me move closer to my vision, or is it keeping me stuck?" You're essentially becoming a scientist of your own mind—collecting data, testing hypotheses, and drawing conclusions based on evidence rather than assumptions.

The best way to practice this kind of discernment is through questioning, and that's exactly what we're going to do next with an exercise that will help you examine your thoughts more critically.

Exercise: Fact or Fiction?

This exercise is inspired by Socratic questioning—the idea that we can discover truth and gain deeper understanding by asking a series of thoughtful, probing questions rather than by simply accepting our initial assumptions. Socrates believed that wisdom comes not from having all the answers, but from knowing which questions to ask. So let's ask better questions that will help you unravel your disempowering thought loops and any biased stories you might be telling yourself.

Here's an example.

You receive a brief email from a parent requesting a meeting with you as soon as possible. Immediately you feel your stomach drop and your palms start to sweat. You breathe your way to a more relaxed state. You investigate what feeling has triggered this physical reaction, and it's definitely a combination of fear and dread. But why?

You do a quick thought scan and see where your attention went right after you received that email and realize you have this disempowering thought: *Student behavior is my weak spot.*

When that thought appears, it floods your mind with negative scenarios and bad outcomes. You look for signs that prove this meeting is going to put you on the defensive—the wording of the email, the punctuation used, the absence of a *sincerely* or a *warm regards* at the end.

To sum it up, the story you tell yourself is "I'm a terrible teacher."

This is where you can interrupt this feedback loop with an important question:

Is this story true or false? Separating fact (the objective truth of what is happening) from fiction (your brain's biased interpretation of what is happening) is how you start breaking the loop.

So let's quickly break it down with a few sample answers.

FICTION: SUBJECTIVELY INTERPRETED (DISEMPOWERING)	FACT: OBJECTIVELY TRUE (NEUTRAL)
A parent wants to confront you about something they think you did wrong regarding their child's behavior. You're not good at your job.	A parent wants to speak with you about something urgent. You don't know what the issue is just yet.

Now that you see that there's a sharp distinction between what your thoughts say (disempowering) from what the situation is (neutral), you can follow that up with a two-part question that will help you dig even deeper.

Who am I when I believe that thought?

Now take a break to regulate, with a cleansing breath or one of the options in chapter 1. Once you've regulated, ask part two of the question: *Who am I when I don't believe that thought?*

Let's break it down again and see side-by-side comparisons of the possible answers:

WHO AM I WHEN I BELIEVE THAT THOUGHT?	WHO AM I WHEN I DON'T BELIEVE THAT THOUGHT?
I'm worried and stressed out. I feel so much pressure and like my job is at stake. My people-pleasing tendencies go into overdrive, and I freak out at the thought of doing something wrong and causing a conflict. I can barely get through my lessons because I'm a nervous wreck.	I'm more confident that I can handle the situation. I might reply and ask for some more details about the discussion they want to have, so I can be fully prepared. I can go about the rest of my day unbothered and teach my students without being distracted by thoughts that don't serve me.

Now you've got a clear picture of how you show up with your disempowering thought that's based on a negative and subjective interpretation versus how you might behave if you do the opposite.

So here's the best part: you get to choose.

You get to decide whether you want to keep this thought.

Because it's entirely up to you. After you regulate your nervous system, if you want to, you can literally just throw the thought away, like a crumpled-up piece of scrap paper.

You just have to replace it with an empowering thought.

DISEMPOWERING THOUGHT	EMPOWERING THOUGHT
I'm a terrible teacher.	I can navigate through the things that are coming my way and ask for help when I need it.

Find a printable PDF version of this exercise at *empowered educator.com/book*.

THE CHOICE IS YOURS

As psychologist William James put it: "The greatest weapon against stress is our ability to choose one thought over another."

We've covered a lot of brain science in this chapter—plenty of anatomy and biology and neurological fun facts. But all that learning is in service of this one simple truth.

You can choose one thought over another.

Remember, your brain wants to keep you alive. And so far, that big, beautiful brain of yours has been doing an amazing job, right? It's got a 100 percent success rate, because here you are, reading this book. So give your brain—and yourself—some credit.

More than that, give yourself some *grace*.

You were more than likely brought up to think that your thoughts run the show (and not the other way around) because your parents and your schoolteachers and *their* parents and *their* schoolteachers and generation after generation have been brought up that way. Even though William James explored the notion that the brain and its systems weren't fixed, but could be shaped by repeated actions, in his 1890 book, *The Principles of Psychology*,[5] the concept of neuroplasticity started to gain notice only in the mid-twentieth century, and then *really* became a topic of scientific research in the 1980s.

But now you know that you don't have to keep going on autopilot. You can change everything when you change your thoughts.

MAIN TAKEAWAYS

- Metacognition—thinking about thinking—allows you to observe your thoughts objectively, question whether they're serving you, and choose different ones.
- Your thoughts and your identity are separate things. When you understand that you *have* a brain (rather than being controlled by it), you can start to exercise agency over your thought patterns instead of feeling powerless against them.
- The limbic system—including your amygdala and hippocampus—evolved to keep you alive by detecting threats, not to help you thrive or feel

fulfilled, and can even overpower your brain's regulatory system when threatened. This means your brain will often resist positive changes because they feel unfamiliar and potentially dangerous . . . but that doesn't make them *actually* dangerous.

- Because your brain can process only a tiny fraction of available information, it selects what to pay attention to based on what you've told it is important through the reticular activating system. Choosing what you're looking for is a supercharged way to use that ability for empowerment.

5

REFLECT TO REFRAME

Back in my teaching days, I had a habit of forgetting my coffee mug in the faculty room sink. On one of those rare moments when I actually remembered to grab it before leaving, I ran into Lauren.

Lauren was a ninth-grade social studies teacher I'd met a few times in passing but didn't know very well. When I saw her sitting alone at a table after school, with a blank look on her face, I had to ask what was up.

"Oh, it's nothing," she said. "It's just . . . I had an admin observation today and I totally blew it."

Naturally I sympathized, and I asked what happened. Lauren went on to describe a litany of mishaps: She forgot to write her objective on the board. She misplaced her folder of worksheets and had to print them out all over again, wasting time as the class got antsier and antsier. The principal didn't smile *once*. And when he did call on one of her students, he happened to pick the one kid who *always* struggled to pay attention in class.

It sounded like she'd had a rough time. I told her I'd totally been there and wished her good luck with her follow-up meeting the next week before scooting off to pick up my kids from school.

A few weeks later, I happened to run into Lauren again by the copy machine, and I asked how her meeting had gone. This time, her face lit up.

Turns out, the principal told her it was one of the best observations he'd ever done. Direct quote.

Lauren seemed both thrilled and a little confused. "I was *convinced* I'd done terribly," she told me, "but apparently I crushed it. Isn't that wild?"

I'll tell you what I told Lauren. Actually it's *not* so wild—it's neuroscience. (Which, admittedly, can sometimes *sound* a little wild when you first learn about it.) The truth is, our brain innately zeroes in on the negative aspects of our experience.[1] When Lauren was in the thick of her observation—and remembering it afterward—her brain was doing exactly what it's wired to do: pick up on the slipups (forgetting the objective), the potentially threatening emotional signals (the unsmiling principal, the antsy students), and the just plain bad luck (calling on the kiddo who struggles to pay attention). It was only *after* the fact (thanks to her meeting with the principal) that she realized just how limited her take on the situation had actually been.

Thankfully, there's a way to work *with* our brain's wiring rather than be trapped by it. Just like metacognition gives us an edge in leveraging our brainpower, reflective thinking is a practice that hones our internal processing skills so when we have new experiences, our minds don't automatically jump to whatever went wrong or resist information that challenges our worldview.

And when that does happen, we can redirect away from

seeing only the negative things from the day (or admin observation). Instead of focusing on those cringeworthy or embarrassing or frustrating moments, we can see things in a less activated state—more consciously and objectively—so that we can proceed in a way that aligns with our vision, not with our default wiring.

When we engage in reflective thinking, we gain the power to rewrite our daily narrative from one of defeat and victimhood to one of growth and possibility. In this chapter, you'll understand why and how your brain seems to cling to the bad parts of your day and why getting stuck in the role you play (a classic pattern for teachers) can hinder your ability to reflect fully. From there, you'll see how you can navigate conflict and stressful situations more easily, and you'll learn a simple four-question framework that will help you interrupt the spiral of negativity, honor the challenging moments, and turn reflection into concrete action steps that move you forward rather than keep you feeling stuck.

THE LENSES WE SEE THROUGH

Our brains are powerful networks, and on a day-to-day basis, they are taking in a *lot* of information. Even with the impressive processing power of the human brain, we simply can't digest every single stimulus we're bombarded with all the time. In order to get anything done (including staying alive), we have to have some sort of system to filter out the news from the noise. In the last chapter we explored the function of the reticular activating system. Now we are looking at the filter of what I call our *interpretive lenses.*

Our interpretive lenses are just what they sound like: the things we look through in order to make sense of the world around us. The same way the lenses in a pair of glasses affect how light hits your eyes and how you make sense of that information, these lenses help our brain interpret a situation, decide what's important, and determine what course of action we should take. And as is true with the lenses in glasses, we rarely look at the interpretive lenses themselves. By nature, they're invisible—they work without our ever thinking about them consciously, because their whole point is to make things more efficient for us. But *because* they're invisible, it's easy for us to forget (or never realize) we have them in the first place.

So let's look at (not through) these lenses and get a solid foundation for our reflection practice.

The Survival Lens

As we discussed in chapter 4, your brain's main job is to keep you alive, and with that as priority one, ancient humans as a matter of survival focused more on stimuli that were dangerous/bad than on those that were safe/good. When the stakes were life and death, we needed a way to be able to notice and dwell on anything that could be a potential threat—one that we could deploy lightning-quick (and subconsciously). This is our survival lens, our way of interpreting the world so that we don't get pulverized by it.

This lens inherited from our *Homo sapiens* ancestors works a little differently in a world where we're not running from predators or worrying about which fruits are poisonous. In modern human life, our survival lens means that the default setting in our mind is to scrutinize all our actions and other people's behaviors instead of observing and learning from them; to make quick judgments rather than really considering whether a given stimulus represents the truth, the whole truth, and nothing *but* the truth—displaying what you might know as a *negativity bias*. Lauren's experience of her administrator's observation is a great example of negativity bias at work. Her nervous system was on the lookout for any potential danger, and using this lens, Lauren found it.

But our survival lens isn't shaped only by the need to protect ourselves from predators. For us humans, it's not simply enough to stay alive (asking, "Am I safe?"); we also want to live as individuals, to self-actualize, to have a real sense of self (asking, "Who am I?").

Enter your ego. The ego is the part of the psyche that creates separation, individuality, and a sense of self. It's what says, "This is mine, and that is yours" and "Here's where you end and I start." It is *also* working to help you survive—in this case, by ensuring your sense of place in the world as an individual. Again, we often think of the ego as a bad thing, considering that to "have an ego" is to be inherently full of yourself, but the truth is, we *all* have an ego, and it's part of how we exist as humans.

But here's the thing about the ego: It loves to be right. If the ego could talk, its catchphrase would probably be "I told you so." When it encounters any new information that *challenges* an existing belief, your ego is like, "Whoa, wait a second!" It activates your fear response and subconsciously gets you thinking that this new information must be wrong, dangerous, or untrustworthy. The truth is, the ego needs to be right in order to feel safe.

This means your survival lens is also fine-tuned for *confirmation bias*: to affirm the things your ego already knows and to push out anything that contradicts that "truth." For example, if someone offers feedback or a different perspective, the unchecked ego interprets this as a threat instead of an opportunity for growth because accepting that information might require rethinking something about yourself. On the other hand, your ego will always accept new information that confirms your beliefs. If you believe that you're no good at technology and you find yourself struggling with new grading software, your bias sees this as confirmation that you're not cut out for this. If you believe you're underappreciated at work, your ego says, "I told you so," when your principal gives praise to someone else at the faculty meeting. It's important to remember that these biases are often subconscious. However, they are what we're going to carry with us by default unless we take the time to reflect and unpack them a bit.

That said, it's not enough to understand how *any* human brain would digest a situation. You want to understand how *your* human brain is interpreting it, making meaning of it, and spurring you into action. And to do this, you need to reflect a bit on who *you* are—to think in terms of another bias your ego and survival lens is responsible for: the *identity bias*.

The *identity bias* is also a way for the ego to feel safe (and therefore keep *you* safe). This is another gift from our *Homo sapiens* ancestors (thank you again!). Back then, belonging wasn't optional—it was a matter of survival. Community meant protection, food, and safety, while isolation meant death. Back then, knowing who you were as an individual opened the door for you to associate with people who were familiar and therefore safe. Since we're no longer living in communal caves, this *identity bias* plays out a little differently.

When I ask teachers to tell me about themselves, the responses are remarkably consistent. "I am a teacher" is usually the first thing that comes out of their mouths. (No surprise there.) Then comes some variety: "I am a dad," "I'm married," "I am a daughter." But what all these answers have in common is that they are *roles*: jobs we do or positions we fill.

Through my own work and research, I've learned that these

really are just parts that we play. Who we *truly* are exists underneath, above, and beyond all those roles. And understanding this distinction is crucial because when we become too attached to a particular role or piece of our identity, we set ourselves up for emotional turbulence when things don't go according to plan.

This is why it sometimes feels devastating when, for example, your students are misbehaving one day. If you're deeply attached to being a "good teacher," your brain immediately jumps to: "If my students are acting up all of a sudden, I must not be doing a good job. Therefore *I'm* no good. What does that mean about my place in the world?" But that's not actually what's happening at all. It's your attachment to that specific identity that's causing you to interpret the situation through such a narrow, self-critical perspective.

The same thing often happens when teachers retire. After decades of defining themselves by their profession, they suddenly ask, "Who am I now if I'm not doing this thing I've always done?" The identity crisis can feel overwhelming because we don't realize we could (or we chose not to) foster the person underneath the roles.

I experienced this firsthand during one of the most challenging periods of my life. A large part of my own self-discovery started during COVID, when everything I thought I knew about myself was stripped away almost overnight. I had just gotten divorced and moved out of my house with my two kids, who were five and seven at the time, the same weekend the world shut down in March of 2020. Suddenly I was no longer a wife. I was no longer living in the familiar space I'd called home. I wasn't teaching in the way I was used to. I couldn't even make music the way I had before—singing itself felt dangerous during those early pandemic days. Everything I thought I was the day before, I suddenly wasn't. It was jarring and disorienting.

That fall, while homeschooling my kids, I decided to start my PhD, and I was grappling with my new identity as a student again. I remember in my first class my professor asked everyone to introduce themselves. Once again, the roll call (role call?) began: One by one, my classmates introduced themselves in relation to their spouse or partner, their children, or their job. When it was my turn, I realized with startling clarity: *I don't know who I am.* Enter more snot-bubbles-coming-out-of-my-nose *sobbing.*

Yes, of course I was still a mom, but I didn't want to lead with that. After lots of crying (followed by lots of breathing), in reflecting on that moment of vulnerability, I discovered something profound—I was actually something underneath all those roles. Who was I when I got to be *just Jen*? Those other things were identities I got to choose, play, and embody, but they weren't the totality of who I was.

This realization completely transformed how I understood the lens of identity. When we become too attached to the stories around our identities, we lose the ability to step back and see situations objectively. We can frame things only through that lens, and we'll *never* let it go.

Let's go back to that situation of those students misbehaving. If you're heavily attached to the identity of being "the teacher whose students are always well-behaved," their behavior becomes an immediate reflection on your worth. Your survival lens hones that information to confirm what you already "know" about yourself (thanks for that, ego), and suddenly this single incident becomes evidence that you're a failure. Over time, these stories then become the "truths" and beliefs we carry about ourselves.

But what if the kids aren't behaving simply because they're . . . kids? What if it has nothing to do with your teaching ability and everything to do with any number of possible external factors—like the fact that it's the day before a holiday or they just came from a pep rally—that have nothing to do with you or your self-worth?

It's not that your kids aren't behaving. It's that your ego is making their misbehavior mean something about *you,* and when the moment becomes all about you and not about what your students might need, you're no longer able to view the situation from a constructive perspective. But when this reflection comes from a place of neutrality, you get to stop taking the situation personally and find a real way forward.

That said, cultivating detachment from these roles-as-identities isn't just about problem-solving in the moment (though it certainly does help weather the storm of a wild day in the classroom). Holding your identity *loosely* is an invaluable practice for your whole life, even beyond your teaching career—because yes, one day even if it's far in the future, you probably won't be teaching in the classroom anymore. Who you are right now is temporary, and your identity is always shifting. Impermanence is the nature of existence.

This might feel uncomfortable to look at head on, but especially as teachers, we know it to be true in so many ways. We see this impermanence and constant change in action year after year. The kids who pile into our classrooms on the first day of school are wildly different from the ones who wave goodbye for summer break. Teeth have been lost, skills have been gained, and friendships have been made. "Our" kids become someone else's—or enter into the real world.

And while *everything is temporary* might sound like some kind of defeatist, resigned, stress management mantra, I promise you it can be quite the opposite. Embracing the impermanence of our lives isn't just about enduring the tough times—the stressful testing weeks, the long red lights, the budget cuts. It's just as much about savoring the good ones. When we say, *This, too, shall pass* when our students are laughing and playing, the lights are green, and our hard work is acknowledged and rewarded, it makes those times that much sweeter. You're there, fully present in that precious fleeting moment, and you're not letting it pass you by without taking notice.

We're all works in progress. And the more you try to hold on to any fixed idea about yourself or your life, the harder it becomes to create meaningful change and the more frustrated you'll feel. Embracing impermanence allows us to exist in alignment not just with ourselves but with everything around us.

It's true that our biology (and our ego) wants us to cling desperately to the things we think keep us safe—particularly our identities. "This is the way it's always been. This is who I am." But tightening our grip, counterintuitively enough, often leaves us with nothing to hold on to at all. Think about when you're at the beach trying to take a fistful of the sand—you can't! The harder you squeeze, the more it flows from your hand. But if you hold your hands gently, relaxed but firm, you can cup some sand for a little while. The same is true for the roles we play: When we learn to hold these identities more loosely, there's fluidity, change, and possibility around us.

The Cultural Lens

It's no surprise that what you're told throughout your life or what is modeled by your elders can have just as powerful an effect on how you see (and judge) the world around you as what you experience firsthand.

For example, when I was growing up, we all knew that my uncle never ate fruit. Ever. And so as a young kid, my cousin assumed (not unreasonably . . . silly, perhaps, but not unreasonable for a little kid) that it wasn't masculine to eat fruit.

That's just what was modeled for her. Years later, when she was in college and dating her boyfriend (who then became her husband), she walked in on him . . . eating some cantaloupe. This absolutely shocked my cousin—a *man* eating *cantaloupe*?! Once the truth came out, they both had a good laugh about it—because yes, men do in fact eat fruit. It sounds ridiculous, but for my cousin it was a moment of totally relearning something she'd taken for granted as fact based on her previous experience in life as a child.

Or to use a personal example, when we were little, my sister, Rachel, and I were both explicitly taught by our mom and dad that when we went to a friend's house for a playdate, we should *never* go into the parents' bedroom. That would be seen as invasive and rude. Fast-forward to our late thirties, when a mutual friend is eager to show us a new outfit hanging up in her closet, and my sister and I both find ourselves hesitating by the door of her bedroom. We looked at each other and asked, in unison, "Is this because of Mom and Dad?" We *still* laugh about that.

While these are relatively lighthearted examples, viewing things through cultural lenses can have deeper repercussions, leading to misjudgment or misunderstanding. For example, suppose a teacher was raised with the expectation that children should look adults in the eye when speaking to them, but a student was raised with the understanding that looking directly at adults is *incredibly* impolite. You can see how both the people in this example can be looking at a situation "correctly" through their own lenses yet still end up at odds with each other.

Culture is one of those abstract words that we all use a lot (especially in education) but never seem to unpack or examine whether we're all talking about the same thing. But when it comes to understanding our lenses, knowing how all the different levels of culture can show up and affect our view of the world is critical, so let's peel back exactly what we're dealing with here.

I like to explore culture using the model in Zaretta Hammond's fantastic book *Culturally Responsive Teaching and the Brain.*[2] She breaks the idea of culture into three different categories: surface, shallow, and deep.

The first one, surface culture, is usually easy for people to understand. These are the aspects of our culture that are for the most part outwardly visible and observable—foods, clothes, holidays—and teachers know what it means to acknowledge these cultural differences (for example, helping accommodate a student who's missing class for religious services, or finding a teachable moment when one student calls another's lunch "weird"). It's the level of culture you might see on display at a festival, a food fair, a "learn about different holidays" pageant—important and valid, but far from *everything* that comprises a culture.

What's really interesting is when we get to shallow and deep culture. Shallow culture is the set of norms we hold true around social scenarios—things like manners, ways of greeting people, and views of time—while deep culture revolves around the highest-stakes scenarios, such as decisions about our health, our relationship with spirituality, and so on. I'll ask for examples of shallow culture from my workshop participants, and one person might say, "Well, where I grew up, we all slurped our noodles because it was a way to show enjoyment of what we were eating."

Then another person might reply, "Wow! *I* was taught to eat as silently as possible! I used to get my dinner taken away if I was too noisy with my spaghetti."

It's an eye-opening and sometimes amusing moment in the workshop (kind of like my cousin's epiphany that men can eat fruit). But imagine how differences in shallow culture can affect what happens in our classroom. If you have a student whose parents have taught them *It's okay to call the trusted grown-ups in your life by their first names,* but you as the teacher are of the belief that *Kids should always address adults as Mr. or Ms. So-and-So,* how is that going to play out? Probably not well.

When we think in terms of metacognition and reflection, having an understanding of cultural identity is huge. It's not that you need to be a walking encyclopedia of social norms; you have an opportunity to acknowledge and remember that culture truly can shape our perception of what's going on. That simple understanding can create awareness that lets you pause and proceed to navigate those situations with curiosity.

The Emotional Lens

No matter how much we might *want* to think of ourselves as rational, logical beings who act purely out of well-reasoned conclusions, we are in fact human. Humans have emotions. And emotions affect how we take in and interpret a situation—our emotional lens.

Like all lenses, our emotional lens isn't inherently bad. Once again, think of the movie *Inside Out* (thank you, Pixar, for giving us such a wonderful tool for explaining some of our inner workings!): The character of Joy comes to realize that all emotions (even Sadness, Joy's polar opposite) have an important role: They help Riley know when she needs to do something differently in life.

We run into problems when we get too stuck in any one emotional lens or simply don't realize that an emotional lens is affecting how we see something. In Riley's head, the emotion characters—Joy, Disgust, Anger, Sadness, and Fear—all have their own perspectives on a situation, but no *one* of them alone represents *everything* about Riley or her feelings. By the same token, your emotional lens in a given moment isn't the *only* way you could *ever* feel about that situation or in general. You are not your emotions; you *have* emotions. When you can instead experience your emotion for what it is but also see *outside* of it to the other lenses you might look through, you can start to cultivate the real flexibility and empowerment that helps you navigate any tough scenario.

Exercise: Trying On a New Emotional Lens

This exercise was taught to me by Carol—my former professor whom you might remember from chapter 1—and it's an excellent one. It's kind of like when you go to the eye doctor and they ask you to read through the different diopters to pinpoint your prescription—*Better one? Or better two?*—except in this case, the lenses are metaphorical.

Next time you find yourself in a challenging moment and feeling disempowered, try adjusting your lens to the lens of different emotions. Ask questions like:

How would ease look at what's going on here?

What would forgiveness do in this situation?

How would joy see this?

What could generosity give me in this moment?

And so on. You might be surprised how easily you can reframe a situation just by swapping the emotional lens. This is about stepping out of yourself and trying on a new perspective. Just this week, while I was writing this chapter, I found myself editing and reediting, and I ended up feeling *super* frustrated. It was hitting on an old perfectionist role I used to identify with. After I did some breathing and regulated my nervous system with a long walk, I chose to look at the situation through the lens of *ease.* I remembered that I *love* to write. I remembered that writing this book began from a place of joy and inspiration. I unlocked an entirely new perspective that made my frustration dissipate because I was no longer spinning an old story: *I need to be perfect.* Instead, I consciously chose a new, empowering story that allowed me to move forward with confidence: *I am doing the best I can, and that is enough.*

The bottom line here is that these lenses aren't good or bad or right or wrong—they just *are*. It's what we do (or don't do) with them that creates problems—usually because we don't recognize that *our* truth isn't *the* truth, and we don't take the time to get curious about someone else's lens.

By the same token, understanding that you have specific lenses that affect how you see things isn't about casting blame or beating up on yourself. It's about cultivating an objective mindset so you can become a nonjudgmental observer and be curious about your thoughts, feelings, and actions . . . which is what reflection is all about. You don't see the world as it is, you see the world as *you are.*

There is so much beauty in that. As we start to realize that *maybe the way I'm seeing it isn't the way that everybody sees it,* we also start to think, *How can I shift my lens so that I can understand the way this other person might be seeing things? How could my lens be overfocusing on some parts of the story and not others? How could my lens be leaving out some things entirely?*

The reflection process in this chapter will help you start to make those shifts, to see the lenses themselves and not just see *through* them. Reflection, as I define it, means practicing perpetual curiosity. The identities we hold, the roles we play, the feelings we have, and the culture in which we've been raised all have a hand in how we see the world. Reflection allows for the opportunity to recast identities, roles, and feelings as lenses, as *versions* of yourself.

Throughout this book, you're learning to release pieces of who you've been to make room for who you want to become. This is the same principle: It's not about abandoning all sense of self, but about knowing yourself so well that you can see how you are much more than just the roles you play and the identities you occupy. It's about seeing yourself truly as a *human being* instead of a *human doing*, or as synonymous with the role you're playing. And when you can do this, hold your various roles and identities lightly enough that they can serve you rather than rule over you, you step into empowerment. When you're no longer (implicitly) approaching situations from a question of "How do I protect my identity as a good teacher?" but rather from questions of "How am I entering this situation? What role am I attached to here? What am I making this mean about me?" you create the space you need to respond rather than react, to see the situation clearly rather than through the narrow filter of a threatened identity.

So what if you could use your lenses—and your growing awareness of them—as a tool to navigate conflict rather than inadvertently fuel it? What if you could hold your identities more lightly, seeing them as points of entry into curiosity rather than fixed truths that must be protected? What if you could allow yourself to understand your emotional lenses without becoming fully enmeshed in them?

That's not only possible—it's transformative. And that's where real reflection and growth can begin.

THE EMPOWERED EDUCATOR REFLECTION FRAMEWORK

Now that you understand how your survival lens, cultural lens, and emotional lens shape your perception, you're ready to put this awareness into practice. The framework below will help you consciously shift these lenses and see a broader and more nuanced version of reality—one that leaves you feeling regulated and empowered, not panicked and stuck.

When I was teaching seventh- and eighth-grade chorus, I had eighty-some middle schoolers in my classroom. That was challenging enough—you have to grab their attention right away or you'll lose them for the duration—but it got even tougher when one year, chorus was moved *right after lunch.*

For that entire September, it felt like everything that could go wrong did. The kids came in all riled up from lunch, energized by food and eagerly relaying drama to each other. I'd run out of sheet music, the office would call in the middle of class to pull a student for the nurse, I'd forget to give an exit ticket. And at the end of every day, my mind would spin with everything that had gone wrong. *That sucked. I should have made more copies. Why did I forget to plan that exit ticket?* This *was a problem, and* this *was a problem, and* this *was a problem . . .*

By October, I was already dreading that class. How could I go on the whole school year like that?

Simple answer: I couldn't. That's when I realized something had to change—not just for me, but for my students, who were caught in the same unhelpful pattern.

I started with a basic question. Instead of dwelling on all the issues, I asked myself: *What went well?* And make no mistake about it, this wasn't an easy question for me to answer at first. But what I realized is that even on the worst days, there was always something: "Nobody got hurt." "We all made it to the end of class." Even sometimes "many students actually participated enthusiastically." The reason this question is hard is because you're forcibly overriding your brain's survival lens—and that's not how you've been wired to think! But by the same token, it's also the most critical question because it defuses the stress, shifts you out of survival mode, and gets you into a more empowering mindset.

Next, when I had settled my nervous system and wasn't grinding it out in fight-or-flight mode, I acknowledged the next question: *What was challenging?* I consciously *didn't* want to phrase this as "What went wrong?" because I knew that would create a slippery slope into a story about my perceived inadequacy as a teacher (or my students' bad attitudes). Here it's easy to let the emotional lens write the narrative. Instead, I wanted simply an objective look at what was hard to do that day.

Then came the big one: *How do I feel?* I had to ask this one third, because I knew I needed my nervous system to regulate (especially after the mega-stimulating experience that is middle school chorus rehearsal) in order to check in with my feelings and not get overwhelmed by them. My answers weren't sugarcoated, either: sometimes I'd simply say, "I'm frustrated and relieved it's over." Naming that feeling was powerful.

At this point, my brain was asking me something like: *Okay, so now what? How do I want to proceed?* Based on what I've learned, what concrete steps could I take? What information was I missing? What questions could I ask? Maybe I could have a student answer the phone so I wouldn't miss a beat (ha!) while conducting. Maybe I could be sure to have extra copies on hand in case new students were dropped into the class. An action item or two to give myself moving forward.

As I adopted this reflection practice, things started to feel smoother for me. But what truly amazed me was watching this same pattern play out with my students. For example, after we'd run through songs for our solo festival, I'd always ask, "How did that feel?" and the first words out of their mouths were some variation of "Well, I forgot the words here, and I didn't breathe where I was supposed to, and I cracked on that high C . . ." Their answers all came through the lens of their ego-driven survival lens—their need to stick to the familiar and known reality.

But after developing my reflection questions, I'd gently interrupt them and redirect: "Let's try this differently. Can we start with what went well?" Watching them learn to interrupt their own negative spirals and find something to celebrate, even in imperfect performances, was one of the most powerful teaching moments of my career.

At its heart, that's what this reflection practice is: interruption. In most contexts, interruption is rude, but in your inner dialogue, it's essential. You have to actively stop the negative spiral before it gains momentum. The moment you notice yourself cataloging everything that went wrong, interrupt that process and reflect instead.

This can feel challenging. Sometimes acknowledging those negative thoughts feels too risky—we tell ourselves they're mean, untrue, disempowering. But here's the paradox: Giving your difficult and disempowering emotions airtime is actually more helpful than trying to bypass them. Those thoughts exist for a reason. They're your brain's way of saying, "We need attention here."

Your job isn't to judge these thoughts or make them go away. It's to notice them objectively: "I'm having the thought that I'm a terrible teacher. Interesting. What does this feeling need from me right now?" Maybe you need to use one of your regulation tools. Maybe you need to scream in your car or punch a pillow. Maybe you need a walk. The key is responding to the need, not just the emotion.

And to be sure, even with this framework, there will be moments when you forget everything you know. Imagine you're building something with a toolbox full of helpful instruments, but suddenly a bear appears. In that moment of pure survival, you can't remember what tools you have, let alone how to use them. Your instincts take over completely.

This is human. This is normal. The bear will eventually leave, and you'll remember your tools again. Everything is temporary, including the moments when you feel most overwhelmed and least equipped. But if you keep your toolbox with you, I promise you'll have another chance to use it the next time around.

The Four Empowered Reflection Questions

You can get the PDF at *empowerededucator.com/book*.

- *What went well?* Asking this question first deliberately overrides your survival lens. (Remember, your brain is wired to look for threats, failures, and other negative confirmation bias first.) Identifying what went *right* gets you unstuck, seeing a more complete version of what actually happened.
- *What was challenging?* This honors the difficulty we may have encountered without shame or blaming ourselves. Instead of your identity lens making a

tough class mean you're a bad teacher, you're simply observing: This particular thing was hard today.

- *How do I feel?* Searching for and naming the emotional lens we're looking through is powerful. Checking in with our feelings gives us the chance to regulate our emotions before we take any further steps.
- *How do I want to proceed?* Deciding what happens next based on our values helps us do better.

With enough practice, you'll be able to mentally run through these questions in real time so you can make more conscious choices that will align with your vision. The best part of mastering reflective thinking as an educator is watching the amazing ripple effect that happens in and out of the classroom.

CURIOSITY CREATES CONNECTION

The four reflection questions are powerful for processing your own experiences. But understanding your own lenses is just the beginning. Recognizing that *everyone* is looking through their own set of lenses can be a powerful tool for understanding and navigating conflict with other people as well. Because, ultimately, so often conflict is simply a result of clashes between two sets of lenses—when you're seeing things one way and someone else is seeing them completely differently. But when you can shift away from "What's wrong with them?" or "Why are they being so difficult?" to "Why might they be looking at things this way?" something remarkable happens.

Here's one example of what that can look like. As the chair of the music department at my school for many years, I was always the spokesperson when things got a little bit . . . complicated. I remember one specific conflict where a certain teacher at the high school—let's call him Joe—was not allowing students to leave his class for their band lessons. So even though I was the middle school choir teacher, as music department chair, I had to talk with this person and find out why his students weren't making their lessons.

When I sat down to listen to Joe, he kept telling me over and over: "Well, it's my time. It's my time. It's *my* time." He was frustrated that the students' excused absences for their band lessons were cutting into "his" instruction time. From his perspective, he was getting shortchanged.

Now, from my perspective—and through my identity lens as the head of the music department—*I* was feeling undermined. These were students who'd chosen, with their families' support, to participate in the music program, and the lessons were a requirement. And with music programs constantly under scrutiny, *especially* when participation is low, I didn't appreciate that these willing and eager musicians were being blocked from their program of choice.

The thing is . . . neither of us was wrong. In fact, I think we were both *right*. But simply standing in our respective corners and insisting on our rightness wasn't going to solve the problem. It might have given each of us a little ego boost, but at the long-term expense of feeling worse overall due to the friction the unresolved conflict would undoubtedly cause.

So I decided to step out of judgment. I actively chose to be curious. Instead of operating from the foregone conclusion that he was blocking my students from participating in the music program, I decided to ask questions. What lens could *Joe* be seeing the situation through?

Now, I didn't know Joe very well, but I knew he taught AP English. That meant his students had Regents exams and AP tests that were quickly approaching. He was up against high stakes, high pressure, and limited time. From that perspective... yeah, I could see why he'd want all the kids in his classroom for every single minute of instruction. Even *that* felt like barely enough time. His lens would focus on these band lessons as just another thing making it harder to succeed at his job.

With that in mind, I reflected on *my* lens. How was I coming at this issue? Well, for me, I identified as someone who values fostering a love of music in students and is committed to high standards of excellence in their craft. I saw in these students a set of kids who had chosen to take on something extra and were committed to pursuing it *in addition* to all their other academic obligations. I knew that these instrumentalists were passionate and dedicated, and often their participation in music ensembles boosts their success in their other academic pursuits. I felt frustrated on their behalf.

That's how I finally hit on common ground.

"I hear you when you say it's *your* time," I told Joe. "I also feel like I'm in a constant time crunch for instruction with our concerts and music competitions around the corner. And I know you have a *lot* on your plate in AP English. It's so hard right now, and I want the students to have everything they need—I mean, we all do, right?"

Joe thought for a moment. Then he nodded.

"But what I keep coming back to," I went on, "is reminding myself that *this is not* my *or* your *time, it's the* students' *time.* And I think that's the angle we have to come at this situation from. How do we help our students make good use of *their* time?"

Again, Joe thought it over. And he agreed to keep talking it through and we were able to navigate to a solution that worked for everyone. In hindsight, it almost sounds simple, finding a way in with the shift of *it's the* students' *time*, but make no mistake: That took a lot of reflection on my part, really peeling back, asking questions, and noticing where my ego was trying to intervene.

A lot of times when there's conflict, it's because there's a perceived difference in values. But notice I say *perceived* difference. When we reflect—when we move from a place of judgment to a place of curiosity—we often discover that our values might not *actually* be so different from the other person's at all. In my case, I was able to tap into the fact that this English teacher and I both shared a pretty powerful value—several, in fact. We both wanted the best for our students. We both wanted to do well in our careers as teachers. And we both understood the pressures of *being* a teacher. Curiosity helped me step back, objectively understand some of the lenses each of us was looking through, see why we *thought* our values were in conflict, and recalibrate to a place of agreement.

Moving from judgment to curiosity—that critical skill for all humans—is particularly valuable for us teachers because there are many, *many* situations where we and the other party are "both right." Education is a uniquely complex field with a lot of stakeholders coming at situations from different perspectives, and if we lock ourselves into judgment, we're liable to get stuck in conflict (at worst) or mired in tension and self-doubt (at best). Remembering instead that we *all* have our lenses and working from that place of *reflection* instead of defensiveness can make all the difference.

MAIN TAKEAWAYS

- Everyone sees the world through a set of lenses—that's part of being human. We don't have to get *rid* of our lenses (that wouldn't be possible!), but we can become aware of them.

- ✦ The roles we play in life can become synonymous with who we are—our identity. That attachment can lead us to make value judgments about ourselves (and our self-worth) when we perceive ourselves as failing to live up to that role. Holding our identities *lightly* can help us from getting too enmeshed and invite curiosity.
- ✦ Thinking in terms of what others' lenses might show them about a situation can be a powerful tool for navigating conflict or even defusing it all together.
- ✦ Reflection can be as simple as asking yourself four questions (in this order): What went well? What was challenging? How am I feeling? How do I want to proceed?

6

COMMUNICATE VALUE

Like a lot of teacher-parents, Sofia spent her days doing double duty with kids—her own and her students—and navigating all their dilemmas, emotions, and challenges. One day, her third-grade daughter came home frustrated. Her teacher had a special, super-cool, cozy reading area set up in one part of the classroom, but every day the same kids would sprint over to it during silent reading time, and Sofia's daughter never got a turn.

"Well, have you told your teacher what you want?" Sofia asked.

Her daughter shook her head.

"Then that might be worth a try," Sofia said. "If there's something you want to change, your teacher needs to hear from you. Otherwise, she might not even realize anything's wrong."

Her daughter gave her a doubtful look—or more accurately, a *Mommmm, are you for real?* look. "But she should just *know*," she groaned. "It's not fair!"

"I know it doesn't feel fair," Sofia replied. "But I bet she'll want to help you find a solution if you speak up for what you want. What if you explained to her what's happening? Maybe she can rotate who gets the reading corner."

Sofia had been working with me for a while, and as we were discussing advocacy in one of my group sessions, she had a lightbulb moment.

"I want my daughter to advocate for herself, especially while in school," she shared. "This whole reading corner thing . . . I was telling her with assurance that this is the way to handle these kinds of situations. But I almost *never* do the same for myself and my classroom."

Throughout your teaching career (and really, throughout your whole life), there are going to be times when you need to advocate: for your students, for your program, for yourself, for your family, for your friends. But advocacy conversations can feel messy—to the point that we often avoid them entirely.

Teachers need to understand how to successfully communicate the value of what we do in order to get the best for our students. We need to be able to demonstrate the impact of our actions: how it's more than just the sum of all our job functions and duties. Advocacy like this is vital!

At the same time, I think advocacy is a little misunderstood. When most people hear *advocacy*, they picture something dramatic: the eleventh-hour rush to a school board meeting, teachers with signs protesting budget cuts, or impassioned speeches to save a beloved program. That's certainly one version of advocacy, but it's not the whole story.

It's true that moments that call for advocacy can feel like high-stakes scenarios—the kind of scenarios where your parasympathetic nervous system checks out, your amygdala checks in, and your body shifts from *performance mode* into *protection mode* right when you need to be at your most articulate and persuasive. Your hands are sweaty, your voice shakes, and you leave a meeting feeling frustrated because you didn't say what you meant to say (or worse, you said something you wish you could take back).

But if you instead remember to keep yourself regulated, *and* you prepare yourself with the right kind of advocacy style—which is what this chapter is all about—you can make real, positive changes happen while staying emotionally in tune.

Depending on the situation, advocacy can fall into one of three camps: reactive, situational, or proactive. I'll break each of these down in this chapter, including when and why we use each type. But regardless of the type, at its core, advocacy is simply communicating value. It's about helping someone understand the importance of something that you already know matters deeply, and enabling them to make an informed decision that takes different perspectives into account.

REACTIVE ADVOCACY

One morning a few years ago, I received some frantic texts from my friend Ella, a forty-year-old middle school teacher in New Jersey. Ella was in between classes when she started venting about her latest work crisis. Three new students—Beatriz, Imka, and Kenneth—had been added to her class without any warning. Beatriz just moved to the area from Portugal and didn't speak English. Imka had some developmental delays and was given an Individualized Education Program (IEP). Kenneth was virtually a mystery because he'd just entered the foster care system from a neighboring county.

I ALREADY have a full class, she texted. *Three new students would be a lot to handle regardless, and these three need extra attention. And I'm already in charge of two after-school clubs on top of this.*

Before I could even type a response, Ella beat me to it.

And yes, I know I have to advocate for myself and these kids, but I'm processing some feelings first.

Usually Ella stayed silent and quietly stewed instead of advocating for herself and her students, so I was thrilled she was starting to take action—and yep, I told her, feel your feelings, and then advocate for what you (and they) need.

Now, I'll be real with you: reactive advocacy sucks. It's the kind of advocacy we jump into when something's suddenly on fire, someone's gotta do *something,* and it's up to us to, well, react.

As such, reactive advocacy comes on the heels of *very* stressful developments: those out-of-the-blue, meteor-strike moments when a policy is announced or a decision has been made and you had *no* idea it was coming (like Ella's surprise new students). Usually, not only were you not at the table when the decision was made, but you didn't even realize there was a table to begin with.

As a result, it can be hard not to get emotional and take what's happening personally. *Why wasn't I consulted? Why are they picking on me?*

That was certainly the case for Ella. She's a gifted and empathetic educator, but in that moment, all she felt was *frustrated.* And when I called her soon after, that's exactly what I heard in her voice.

"I feel like they're singling me out because I'm always so accommodating," she told me. "I never complain, I'm always the team player . . . and now it's biting me in the butt."

Valid feelings . . . and possibly even true. Letting out those emotions is a necessary first step, and critical to ensuring you don't ignore what you're feeling. Ella told me she'd taken some time to Stop and Notice (and do some box breathing) and blocked out some time to draft an email to the principal. Together we worked through her reactive advocacy plan.

First, she needed to clearly articulate the problem. It's very easy—especially when we're in that activated state—to jump into the situation with *our* problems. That's what Ella did when texting me: *This is unfair—I already have a full class! They're just taking advantage of me because they know I won't complain!* Often, this can manifest in our response as passive-aggressive phrases ("I'm not sure why I was not consulted on this, but . . .") or an airing of our grievances ("Frankly, I feel blindsided, and . . ."). It's so tempting to sneak these into our arguments as an extra jab to make, but ultimately, such language is going to be counterproductive. Instead, Ella stated her problem like this: *I see that three new students with high support needs have just been added to my class. This creates some challenges we need to address.*

Next, Ella needed to set out a justification for why things need to change. Once again, this is a beautiful opportunity to demote your ego, lead with your heart, and remember that your focus always needs to be on what's best for kids. Think of setting up the problem in terms of *communicating value*. This means using the language of the people you're addressing.

Consider who sits across from you at that table. What keeps them up at night? What are their priorities? If you're talking to your principal, they're likely focused on student outcomes, budget constraints, and district compliance. They want to hear about learning objectives, data, and solutions that work within existing systems. So instead of saying, "This has to change because it's unfair to me," try "This has to change because it's going to shortchange students in A, B, or C ways." Or "the students will be more successful when X, Y, or Z happens."

It's also important to consciously look for our own blind

spots: Something that may seem *super* obvious to us (through our lenses) might not look that way (or might not even be on the radar) of the person on the other side. When we remember what they might *not* know, it's that much easier to meet them with curiosity instead of judgment and have a productive interaction.

By clearly articulating the problem, Ella had her work cut out for her here. She was able to say: *With twenty-eight students currently in my class, I'm concerned that Beatriz, Imka, and Kenneth won't get the individualized attention they need to succeed. I know how important it is for our school to demonstrate strong performance in serving our students with special needs and ESL students, and a large class size like this works against that goal.*

Finally, the most important tip I had for Ella was to suggest solutions. The honest truth is we can't expect the people who created the problem to solve it for us. In their eyes, they've already chosen the optimal way to go about things, after all . . . and they might not have the time or inclination to go back to the drawing board. Offering a concrete alternative saves them (and you) the time they'd take to deliberate (if they even bother to at all).

Notice that I also say ***solutions***, plural, because offering several choices not only gives you the best odds of hitting on *something* that works, but also signals that you're here to brainstorm, compromise, and collaborate. It's less a "my way or the highway" approach and more of a "here's a road map with a few routes to our destination."

Ella brainstormed three potential solutions. Plan A: Have the students reassigned to teachers with smaller class sizes. Plan B: Get additional paraprofessional support in her classroom for the remainder of the semester, such as a student teacher, a TA, or a dedicated ESL instructor. Plan C: Hand off her extracurricular obligations (such as after-school clubs) to another teacher for the rest of the semester.

As we worked through her approach, I could sense Ella starting to feel defensive again—and I heard in her voice that she was tensing up. I asked her what was coming up for her, and she sighed.

"I just hate that *I* have to come up with the solutions here," she told me. "I'm already doing my job, and now I have to do theirs, too?"

It is *so* easy to fall into defensive mode when we're doing this sort of reactive advocacy. We feel as if we need to be right. Our egos need to make sure that we're holding on to some sort of control. However, at the end of the day, again, this is not about you . . . and you never really had control over *everything* (only over yourself and your actions).

I gently reminded Ella that when you start feeling defensive, it's a signal to pause, regulate your nervous system, feel your feelings as they come up, and shift into curiosity mode instead of resentment mode. Plus, it's another good reason to have more than one plan: If we have only one way to get what we want, and we don't get it, we're just going to retreat into ourselves.

So if you notice those defensive feelings rising up, regulate your nervous system and start to ask questions. The more questions you ask, the better your chances of finding common ground. Curiosity opens doors for genuine communication and conversation, whereas defensiveness creates an "I'm right, you're wrong" standoff. We don't have time for that kind of power struggle. Remember, there's a fire burning! We need to put it out quickly and as effectively as possible. Questions like "From your perspective, what's in the way of making this happen?" or "What would you need to make something like this work?" are always going to be more helpful than digging in your heels.

Two days later, Ella texted me with an update. Her principal had been receptive—*really* receptive. She'd agreed to move Kenneth to a different classroom that had more space. The ESL instructor would spend two periods a week in Ella's room to support Beatriz's transition. And another teacher would co-lead one of Ella's after-school clubs to take some of the time pressure off.

It wasn't everything Ella had hoped for, but it was a workable solution that addressed the core problem: ensuring all students could receive appropriate support while keeping class sizes manageable. More than that, Ella had proven to herself that she *could* be a successful advocate—for herself *and* for her students. Perhaps most important, however, Ella was putting into practice a skill set that we can then model for our students—whether they see us using it or not.

After working with me and implementing these strategies, one middle school teacher shared how much she found in common with a new personal-responsibility framework that her school was encouraging her to teach her students. "It's all the same thing!" She laughed. "Us *and* the kids—we all need this." She's absolutely right. Just like we expect kids to take ownership of their actions and propose solutions rather than just complaining about consequences, we can hold ourselves accountable to be hands-on and forward-focused—even in these fire-drill moments.

Overview: Reactive Advocacy

For times when a problem needs solving *now*—or very soon.

The emotional response:

- *Why wasn't* I *consulted?!* It's not about you. Demote your ego and reconnect to what matters.
- *I feel blindsided.* Valid feeling, but not an argument to do things differently. Think in terms of value to the students.
- *This isn't fair.* Get curious, not defensive. What barriers might be in the way to a workable solution, and how can you co-navigate them with decision-makers?

The strategy development:

- Articulate the problem.
- State the justification.
- Offer solutions yourself (ideally at least a Plan A, Plan B, and Plan C).
- Ask good questions.

SITUATIONAL ADVOCACY

Marcus, a computer science teacher in a rural community, had been building something incredible at his school. As the only certified CS teacher in his district, he'd created an entire standards-based sequence of classes for middle schoolers—a complete career pivot from his previous fifteen years of teaching math. The robotics elective he'd spearheaded in particular was a consistently popular choice for STEM-inclined students.

"It really feels like this is what I was meant to teach all

along," he told me. "And the kids are loving it, too. I mean, who doesn't want to build robots all day?"

The problem for Marcus was that technology moves fast. While he could teach effectively from a math textbook that was a few years out of date, robotic equipment was a different story. The equipment that he'd purchased just over a decade ago still functioned on a *mechanical* level, but as the years passed, more and more companies had sunsetted the *software* support, making the bots effectively useless.

"It's like going to the Geek Squad and asking them to fix your PalmPilot," Marcus explained. "They just don't do that anymore."

It was late November when Marcus and I chatted, and Marcus's principal had asked him to come in after the holidays to state his case for new equipment and software. Unlike Ella's crisis with the surprise students, Marcus had time to prepare. This wasn't a fire that needed immediate attention—it was a moment for situational advocacy.

Situational advocacy is when things aren't actively burning down, but we want something to change. Maybe it's a schedule adjustment, a curriculum update, a staffing shift, or in Marcus's case, a technology refresh. The beauty of situational advocacy is that, while you have a deadline, you still have (comparably) much more *time*: time to research, to build a compelling case, and to approach the conversation strategically.

As we brainstormed, Marcus was overflowing with great stories about how much his students enjoyed the elective, telling me the triumphant tales of how Kinsley and Maria had team-debugged a problem with their rover or how Devon had gone from "I hate math" to staying after school to program a shape-drawing bot. While it was clear Marcus *also* loved the classwork, he definitely knew that this was all about the students, not him.

However, at a certain point, I asked him to pause. "These stories are great," I told him (because they were!). "But—"

"But I need more than that, don't I?" Marcus sighed, and I nodded.

He was right. The most powerful tool you can bring to a situational advocacy conversation? Data.

While stories matter enormously—and we'll definitely use them—numbers often speak louder than narratives, *especially* when you're asking for budget dollars or resource reallocation. At the end of the day, administrators need concrete evidence to justify their decisions to school boards, superintendents, and taxpayers, and usually, that evidence needs to be something that fits in a spreadsheet.

Fortunately, as a math guy, Marcus was more than game to quantify things. But even as he started brainstorming some ways to show the value of the elective in black-and-white, I could sense some hesitation brewing.

"It just bums me out that I have to beg like this," he said. "I feel like if I was actually doing a good job with this elective, I wouldn't even have to ask. They should *know* that I am a great teacher and trust me that this upgrade was worthwhile. Maybe I'm just not doing enough."

This is where situational advocacy can go sideways fast.

Let's be clear: Your self-worth is never up for negotiation. *Never.* There is no world where you allow someone else to decide whether you're valuable. Marcus wasn't advocating for his worth as a teacher or a person—he was advocating for his program's needs. (More on this later.)

This distinction matters more than you might think. When we conflate our personal value with the thing we're advocating for, our language changes, our emotions shift, and suddenly we're not talking about outdated robots anymore—we're talking about respect and recognition, about whether we matter.

That's a much harder conversation to have productively (and can be ineffective in your advocacy efforts).

So I guided Marcus through the same reframe I often share: This isn't about you. It's about the students and what they need. With that mindset shift, Marcus felt better equipped to tackle his prep time, and he promised to keep me updated.

Over the next few weeks, Marcus dove into data collection. First, he looked into the ***cost data***: what he was asking for and how much it was going to cost. He researched several different educational software companies and their offerings and broke down not only the cost of equipment vs. software, but also the year-over-year cost (since a lot of companies had switched to operating on a subscription model).

Cost data is critical to situational advocacy because more often than not, "How much money do you want?" is going to be the first question—and you want to be prepared to answer it. Having those figures ready to go *and* clearly broken down shows that you've done your homework and are presenting a request that's grounded in the reality of what things cost (and not just a number pulled out of thin air). Even better, Marcus's look into a variety of software providers was a version of that Plan A, Plan B, and Plan C that Ella came up with: a way to preload the conversation with options and set the stage for compromise.

Next, Marcus pulled together some ***context data***. These are facts and figures explaining why this request matters—why it matters now, why it matters here, and why it matters in terms of the desires and goals of the people you're asking. Marcus looked up statistics on coding job growth in their state (projected 15 percent increase over the next five years, compared to 8 percent for all other occupations). He found research showing that students who took computer science in middle school were three times more likely to pursue STEM courses in high school. He even discovered that their neighboring district had just received a $50,000 grant for technology education—proof that funding was available and that other schools were prioritizing this work.

Context data helps administrators see how your request fits into the bigger picture they're accountable for. By connecting his program to broader trends (like job market demands, educational research, and competitive positioning), Marcus showed that this wasn't just about fixing old equipment; it was about improving the students' chances for success *and* improving the school's profile to boot.

Finally, Marcus put together some ***impact data***: evidence of what his program had already accomplished and what it could achieve with better resources. This is where he went back to his students' stories . . . but not just as one-off anecdotes. Instead, Marcus transformed his students' ***qualitative*** experiences into ***quantitative data.*** Basically this means taking the stories and observations he was already collecting and finding ways to assign numbers to them. It's one thing to tell the story of how former math hater Devon got so invested into his robotics project; it's another to say that "nine out of ten students who take this class say it makes them feel more confident in their math skills." And it's not either/or: *Both* pieces come together to paint a compelling picture. All Marcus had to do was ask his kids some basic survey questions and compile their responses into clear data points.

MAKING NUMBERS COUNT: COMPELLING WAYS TO PRESENT YOUR DATA

"Numbers don't lie" (as the saying goes), but sometimes they can be a little dull. As you present your quantitative data, here are some tools you can use to make sure the numbers in question don't feel empty or hollow, but compelling and attention-getting. Pick the one that best fits your situation:

- **Choose the "bigger" number.** Which sounds like more to you, *85 percent* or *17 out of 20*? (I see you shaking your heads, math teachers!) It's true that *numerically* these are equal, but psychologically? Not quite. We subconsciously think *Eight is bigger than seven* and are much more impressed by the percentage than by the raw number. Use that to your advantage!
- **Think of the dentists.** On the flip side, sometimes a smaller but more "human" number is more compelling, for the simple reason that we don't like thinking of people as percentages. Remember those old ads that claimed that "nine out of ten dentists" recommend a specific toothpaste? They wouldn't have worked nearly as well if they'd said "90 percent of dentists agree," so the phrasing was by design. To use that human element to your advantage, choose "X out of Y" figures instead of percentages.
- **Leverage comparisons.** This could look like year-over-year improvement ("student engagement increased from 65 percent to 90 percent"), us vs. them ("our neighboring district just invested $50,000 while we're still using 2014 equipment"), or abstract averages vs. individual schools ("the average student doesn't have the option to take robotics until high school, while our students can start in sixth grade").

- **Weird numbers look more legit.** A quoted cost of $584 sounds more credible and accurate than $550. Why? A round number inherently seems ballparked, while a more specific one implicitly suggests you really crunched the numbers.

- **For the cost of a cup of coffee . . .** We're all wise to those fundraising appeals, but the fact is, they work. Breaking down costs to a per-student, per-year, or even per-day amount will always get you a smaller number than the total (of course), and can reframe a big, unwieldy total into something bite-size and manageable. In other words, try asking not for a $3,500 investment, but for $25 per student (or better yet, $26!).

In summary, when building a case for situational advocacy, you have three types of data at your disposal: cost, context, and impact. Together, these create a complete picture that administrators can actually use to make decisions.

Three weeks later, Marcus walked into that meeting with a folder full of evidence. He didn't lead with "I'm so frustrated with our equipment" or even "We need new software." Instead, he opened with: "I'm so excited to share what our CS classes have been doing, and I'm eager to discuss how we can build on that success."

He started with his impact data—enrollment numbers (up 40 percent over two years), student engagement metrics (95 percent of students said they'd recommend the class to a friend), and concrete examples of how current equipment limitations were holding back student projects. Then he layered in his context data, showing how their program's growth aligned with state job projections and highlighting that neighboring district's recent $50,000 technology grant. Finally he presented his cost data, those three specific options with exact pricing that gave his principal clear choices to move forward.

Halfway through the presentation, his principal looked up from the papers and said, "Marcus, can I admit something to you? I was not looking forward to this conversation. Usually I'm sitting here trying to figure out how to explain why we can't afford whatever a teacher is asking for, and I hate saying no to good teachers. But this really gives me something to work with. There's a lot of clarity here."

In the end, with his principal's buy-in, Marcus got approval for a phased equipment upgrade over two years. It wasn't a landslide win, but it would definitely solve the problem over time, and he'd already laid the groundwork to advocate for more down the road.

The key to Marcus's success wasn't just the data he brought, either. It was how he separated his personal investment in the program from the program's actual needs and used *that* to guide and shape his advocacy. When we can do that separation, our advocacy becomes clearer, more compelling, and ultimately more effective.

Overview: Situational Advocacy

For times when you want something to change but have time to build your case.

The emotional response:

- *They don't value what I'm doing—which means they don't value me.* Your self-worth is never up for negotiation. This isn't about whether you're valued—it's about whether your program gets what it needs.

- *I shouldn't have to prove this is important.* Fair feeling, but proof is power. The more evidence you bring, the easier you make it for administrators to say yes.
- *Why do I have to do all this work to get basic support?* Because you're the expert on what you need, and you're in the best position to make the case.

The strategy development:

- Research cost data (what you're asking for and realistic pricing options).
- Gather context data (why this matters now, here, and to your audience's priorities).
- Gather impact data (what you've already accomplished and what better resources would enable).
- Present all three types together to create a complete, compelling case.

PROACTIVE ADVOCACY

Of all three advocacy styles, this might be the most fun. In fact, you might already be engaging in it—you just didn't realize it.

For example, a teacher I was working with shared that one of her professional goals for that year was to make at least two positive contacts with families per week.

"It's such a joy to tell parents how kind their student was or how hard they've been working on a skill," she confided. "How could you not enjoy sharing that kind of news? And what's wild is that there's this *shift* in my mindset when I look at my students for all the good that they demonstrate. It makes even the observation part of the equation fun. I thought it'd be hard to crank out two of these contacts per week, but now I'm doing as many as five or six."

That's exactly what proactive advocacy is about: highlighting, showcasing, celebrating, and honoring the beautiful work you're already doing every single day. Unlike reactive advocacy (fire-drill mode) or situational advocacy (building a case for something specific), proactive advocacy is about creating ongoing visibility for your program, your students, and your impact.

The beauty of proactive advocacy is that it doesn't require special skills or even that much extra time—just intention and a little bit of action. It's less about *doing one more thing* and more about *cheerleading for things that are already happening.*

Here are some approaches that teachers have found both manageable and effective:

Make the invisible visible. Some of the most amazing things happening in your classroom never leave your classroom. Start documenting and sharing! One teacher shared that she takes photos of any and all events in her classroom, no matter how small (from a pre-K Thanksgiving dinner to students finally reaching fifty books read together as a classroom), and sends them to her district's PR person for inclusion in her district's parent page.

Here are some ideas about things to share:

- Photos of your current classroom setup to highlight curriculum topics
- Student art projects or creative writing assignments
- Quotes from your students in response to a prompt ("What's your favorite thing we learned this week?")
- The aftermath of a big, messy project or a lively time at recess. Sure, finished projects and tidy desks are lovely, but paint-splattered smocks or a pile of jackets and rain boots can speak volumes about how active your students are on the day-to-day.

Connect with your community. Chances are, there's at least one local news outlet in your district. Those outlets *always* want positive stories, especially about kids doing awesome things—and *you* have them!

This is something I used to do all the time. Whenever we had an exciting music program going on or an upcoming concert, I would go to the local radio station and say, basically, "Hey there, I'd love to talk to you about this great new thing we're doing with our students!" They'd then either have me on the air for an interview or push the information about the event to other platforms for more visibility.

It can really be just that easy! Most local reporters are juggling multiple beats and tight deadlines, and when you hand them a ready-to-use story with compelling visuals and clear details, you're solving their problem while highlighting your students' achievements.

To save *yourself* time, I suggest creating a simple media kit that you can adapt for different occasions. Include a one-paragraph description of your program or event, two to three high-quality photos of students in action (with permission forms signed, of course), a brief quote from you about why this matters, and your contact information. For upcoming events like concerts or showcases, send this information two to three weeks in advance, under a clear subject line like "FOR IMMEDIATE RELEASE: Local Middle School Students Showcase Coding Skills at STEAM Night."

Here are some ideas about things to share:

- Student competitions and awards
- Performance events (concerts, plays, talent shows)
- Community service projects
- School or class milestones (100th day of school, reading goal achievements, etc.)
- Seasonal and cultural celebrations

Engage families as partners, not just audiences. Move beyond "your child is doing well" communications and get personal (in a good way). One Spanish teacher told me that she loves to let parents know anytime she hears a student use Spanish outside of class—not for a grade or extra credit, but just to practice or have fun with what they've learned. "I want parents to know that I see that, and I *love* to see it," she said.

Connection matters because parents (and other caregivers) are the other major adult figures in your students' lives—they don't need to feel like strangers. But more than that, parents can be powerful co-advocates for you in reactive or situational cases. They, too, are on the side of the students, and their voices are invaluable. But they are much more likely to collaborate with you and rally around a cause if they already know you *and* what you're engaging their kids in doing day to day.

Here are some ideas about connecting with parents or caregivers:

- Ask parents to contribute expertise to your lessons. Invite the parent who's an engineer to talk about bridge design, or the grandparent who speaks another language to share cultural stories.
- Invite families to see learning in action, not just final presentations. Open your classroom during a "regular" day of instruction for parents to come and join.
- Be specific when sharing how students are growing (e.g., "Maria asked this really thoughtful question today . . ." rather than "Maria is participating well in class.")

Again, the key to sustainable proactive advocacy is building it into routines you already have. You don't need to create a whole new system—just add intentional sharing to things you're already doing:

- If you already take photos of student work, send a few to your principal, school board, or district communications person each week.
- If you already email parents regularly, include one specific positive observation per message.

- If you already attend faculty meetings, occasionally share a quick student success story when it fits the discussion.
- If you already post on the school's approved social media, include classroom moments that showcase learning. And if your school already has channels for sharing like a private social media network or a newsletter, then no need to reinvent the wheel—contribute there, too. (Of course, always follow your district's guidelines and ensure you have permission to share anything you're circulating publicly.)

Proactive advocacy is more of a habit or practice than a one-off project, but it can lead to concrete, specific changes. Sharing the positive things happening in your classroom builds what I call "advocacy capital"—goodwill, awareness, and community investment that you can draw on when you need material or time-bound support later. It's a kind of consistent, strategic relationship building. When budget discussions come up, when schedule changes are proposed, when new initiatives are being considered, the people making those decisions will take that relationship you've forged with your advocacy into consideration.

That's the real power of proactive advocacy: It shifts the conversation from "Can we afford to support this?" to "How can we afford not to?"

Overview: Proactive Advocacy

For creating ongoing visibility and building community support for your work.

The emotional response:

- *I don't have time for self-promotion.* This isn't about you—it's about making your students' learning visible and building support for your program.
- *It feels awkward to brag about my students.* Reframe it as advocacy for your students and your profession. You're showing the world what excellent teaching looks like.
- *Does anyone even care about what goes on in my class?* You'd be surprised! Communities are hungry for positive education stories, and families want to feel connected to their children's learning.

The strategy development:

- Document and share the amazing things already happening in your classroom (make the invisible visible).
- Build relationships with local media to leverage their wide reach.
- Connect with families over the small, personal things as well as the major milestones.
- Present to decision-makers when things are going well, not just when there's a problem.

AVOIDING ADVOCACY PITFALLS

"They just don't value me at work."

I've heard more teachers say this than I can count. Honestly *I've* said it more than once (maybe a *lot* more than once) myself throughout my teaching career. While it's relatable, it's also a mindset pitfall that can seriously shortchange your advocacy.

When you go into an advocacy conversation, as I've said before, it's very easy to make it about you: your passion, your dedication, your value. And it's very easy to feel like this is a good thing, a necessary thing: The topic feels personal to you, so you need to express that as part of your advocacy.

I know all too well what this feels like. Teaching music was something that I wanted to do my whole life, and I spent years completely enmeshed in my identity as a music teacher. So when budget time came around, along with the announcement that they were chopping three and a half positions—which meant no more orchestra, no more choral electives, and no much-needed new instruments—I took it as more than just an insult to the music program; it felt as if *my worth* as a human being was on the line.

What would happen is that I'd advocate for what I *thought* was my department, my program, or my students. But really, I was trying to convey my worth as a person and as an educator to somebody else in order to get them to affirm my value.

This is a major, if well-intended, stumbling block in advocacy that many of us fall into. When you conflate your self-worth with how your community sees and values you—and by extension, what you're advocating for—and the person on the other side *doesn't* see the value, you're just asking for your self-worth to be torn to shreds.

So take a deep breath, regulate your nervous system, and take a step back.

As I said to Marcus, your worth is never up for negotiation. You woke up this morning? Amazing—you're worthy. You're valuable. You're already winning. Separating yourself and saying, *Okay, my being a great teacher, a great mentor, a valuable member of this community? That's not what we're talking about here* is critical. Until you recognize and remind yourself of that, especially going into these advocacy conversations, you're never going to be as effective as you can be.

Second, remember that advocacy is about *communicating.* After you remind yourself of what you're *not* debating, tune into what you *are* about to discuss and reinforce the distinction: *We're talking about money, about communicating the value of the program, about community. None of these things have to do with whether I'm good enough.* That's the switch that needs to happen.

To be clear, this is not about pushing past any emotion to quickly get to a reframe. This is a major case of *Two things can be true at the same time.* I'm inviting you to affirm that, yes, it's not about you, while *also* acknowledging that it *feels* personal. So when those feelings arise? You feel them fully—because that's what your body is asking you to do. Yes, feeling these feelings might be painful, uncomfortable, or frustrating. But when you're able to sit with those emotions and process them fully on your own, you'll be that much more articulate, calm, and well-reasoned in those advocacy spaces. Your sympathetic nervous system (the fight-or-flight response) will not be overriding your prefrontal cortex (the part of the brain responsible for logical argument and rational thinking), and you'll be able to state your case brilliantly and with a level head.

During these high-stakes conversations, check in with yourself—What is my body doing right now? Am I sweating? Is my heart beating fast?—and respond with curiosity and neutral observation. *Okay, I'm activated. That's so interesting.*

Let me take a moment to regulate. This can be as simple as getting back into your body and out of your head by putting your hand on your heart, gently tapping your thigh, or even excusing yourself for a minute to do a quick breathing exercise. Then give yourself the reminders that you need: *This isn't about me. I'm worthy regardless of the outcome here. What do I need to feel and think right now in order to feel well-equipped for this conversation?*

In fact, did you know that in many Romance languages, the word for *lawyer* is related to the English word *advocate: un avocat* in French, *un abodago* in Spanish? (Although in French, it can also mean an avocado, so context clues are important!) I like to remember this little linguistic fun fact because it can help you to think of yourself as a lawyer in these situations. You're preparing evidence, gathering facts, thinking of what will convince the *other* person. Your success in advocacy is not about you, specifically whether *you* are good or deserving. It's *much* more a question of how well you gathered the facts and presented your case. And by the same token, successful advocacy isn't about rewarding the people who are most passionate—*pick me because I care the most* is a convincing argument only on *The Bachelor*!

So process your feelings, find your calm, and present your case. You've got this.

MAIN TAKEAWAYS

- Remember, your worth is never up for negotiation. Instead, advocacy is about clearly communicating the value of programs, resources, or changes that benefit students and the broader educational community.

- Strong emotional responses are normal when confronted with the need for advocacy, especially when you feel blindsided or undervalued. The key is to process those feelings fully before entering the conversation, then approach advocacy from a calm, regulated state.
- Immediate crises like unexpected policy changes call for *reactive advocacy*, planned requests like equipment upgrades call for *situational advocacy,* and ongoing "important but not urgent" relationship and visibility building call for *proactive advocacy.*
- Save time for the decision-makers: Presenting several concrete options (Plan A, Plan B, Plan C) and concrete data (on cost, context, and impact) can make advocacy conversations smoother, speedier, and more satisfying for everyone involved.

7

SPEAK WITH INTENTION

"Sticks and stones may break my bones, but words will never hurt me." My fifth-grade teacher Mrs. Jones used to say this whenever I complained to her that Becky Fraser was teasing me. Even though I was only eleven, I could tell Mrs. Jones meant well. She was trying to teach me how to be resilient and cope in the face of Becky's mean-girl cruelty.

But looking back on it now from an (empowered) educator's perspective, I can't believe how in the dark we all were about the effects words have on people, especially children.

For example, when people are subjected to harsh words, the neural structures that make up the pain matrix in their brain light up. It's why in a heated argument, when the other person delivers a harsh verbal blow, we might notice a sharp twinge in our chest or behind our shoulders. That physical reaction isn't just a phantom psychosomatic pain. It's 100 percent the result of our brains processing the demeaning language and tone of voice being used against us.

In other words, language can actually trigger pain responses in our bodies.

Or in *other* other words . . . You were wrong, Mrs. Jones!

While we communicate in many different ways, language is a powerful tool for changing how we feel because it can be so flexible, rich, and evocative.

So just imagine what it could look like to channel this power for *good*—to help us feel *more* aligned with what we want, and *less* entrenched in what brings us down.

This isn't just about thinking positive or repeating cutesy feel-good slogans, and it's *definitely* not about complaining, venting, and gossiping (which we will get to). What it *is* about is how the words you use every day can in fact keep you in lockstep with your mission and vision—and how easy it can be to make that happen.

Let's go back to Mrs. Jones for a minute. Yes, she had it wrong with sticks and stones (as did a lot of other people back then), but I think she also on some level understood the power we all have to change things.

Mrs. Jones loved to embroider, and she hung up framed pieces of her work on the walls. Some were beautiful flowers or adorable animals, but there were also quotes and sayings. One of them, a gem I never forgot, was this:

The best way to predict the future is to create it.

Yes. In that, Mrs. Jones, you were so, *so* right.

Our language is one of the greatest tools we have for creating that future we want, but that can happen only if we decide we're going to show up for *ourselves* in our words and actions.

So what if you could leverage the words you use to attract new possibilities, connect with your students, and create a community of colleagues that lifts you up?

THE SCIENCE OF LANGUAGE: HOW WORDS WORK (ON US!)

Before we dive into all the ways we can shift our language to feel more empowered, let's establish *how* language has an impact on us. The words we use affect us on a physical, a mental, and an inter/intrapersonal level. Extensive research has been done on this topic, and the results are fascinating. (We'll even try some thought experiments along the way to test the findings out for ourselves.) For now, let's explore the impacts in each of these three domains.

Physical

When it comes to describing the physical manifestations of our feelings, English has a lot of delightfully odd metaphors, from *butterflies in the stomach* to *heart in your throat* to *getting cold feet.* Many of those phrases, however, aren't just cute figures of speech; they're actually rooted in what our bodies do in different circumstances.

For example, when you say you have butterflies in your stomach, you're actually describing the very real sensation that happens when your nervous system redirects blood flow away from your digestive system during times of stress or excitement, creating that fluttery feeling. Having your heart in your throat doesn't mean your circulatory system's gone haywire, but that you're more aware of your pulse as your body slips into a fight-or-flight stage. And you literally get cold feet when you're nervous—your body redirects blood to your vital organs (and away from your extremities) to protect itself.

Even when it gets fanciful, the language we use to talk about our physical feelings is more precise than you might think. The reverse is just as true, too: the way we talk or think (as we learned in chapter 4) about what we're feeling *changes how our body responds.*

One study found that participants who labeled their emotions during a stressful task (a math problem) experienced a lower heart rate than the participants who didn't put words to their feelings (math teachers, take note!).[1] Another study found that labeling feelings out loud during an exposure therapy session, such as an encounter with a spider, significantly reduced physiological arousal (e.g., sweating, heart rate) compared to speaking unrelated words or not speaking at all.[2] Research has even suggested that using certain words and language patterns can predict stress-related changes in our bodies at the genetic level—rewiring our bodies' immune function.[3] How cool is that?!

> **Mini-Experiment:** See what happens to your body when you say the words *joy*, *love*, and *connection*. Likewise, notice what happens when you say *grief*, *resentment*, and *hate*. How does it feel? What happens to your breathing, your heart rate, your muscles?

Mental

Words, like all stimuli, are processed in the brain, so it's not surprising that language has effects on the neurological level. What *is* surprising is what that looks like.

According to one study, encountering action words (like *kick* or *grasp*) activates the same parts of the brain that we'd use to *do* those same actions.[4] On a neurological level, your brain can't distinguish between hearing, reading, or talking about an action and actually *doing* it—that's how powerful a word can be. (And why visualization can work so beautifully, as we learned in chapter 2.)

Choice of words can also affect how we feel about a problem or situation. You've probably said you're *drowning in grading* or *fighting an uphill battle with administrators* or *putting out fires all day,* but have you ever thought about what those figures of speech are telling your brain about the reality of what you're actually dealing with? One study contrasted people's reactions to two versions of a (fictional) news article reporting on crime. One version described crime as a "beast," while the other characterized it as a "virus." Readers were more likely to support increased police intervention after reading the "beast" version, but more likely to support social reforms and inquiries into root causes when crime was called a "virus."[5] Given how often we use metaphors and figures of speech—about one metaphor every twenty words, according to researchers—this is a *huge* revelation.[6]

Then of course there's the good old reticular activating system. Remember, your mind works kind of like Google: Type "anything but cows" into the search bar and you'll get . . . results about cows. By the same token, if you tell your brain, "Don't think about pink cows," you'll find it hard to think about anything *but* pink cows.

This is important because we often think we're asking for what we want, but we're actually focusing on what we don't have. If you say, "I don't have enough time," you're telling your brain you don't have time. If you say, "I wish I was less stressed," you're focusing on stress. If you say, "I wish there was more money in my bank account," you're focusing on not having enough money.

When we flip the script and create language aligned with what we want, we start to see shifts. We're playing with the reticular activating system. When we speak, it goes to work. If you focus on lack and scarcity, that's all your brain will see. If you focus on abundance and gratitude, you'll see and attract more.

> **Mini-Experiment:** Think of an issue or problem you've been struggling with. What happens if you call it something different—an opportunity, a chance to regroup, an invitation for growth? Does that reveal any new ways of approaching it? How do you feel about it now?

Inter- (and Intra-) Personal

An English teacher friend of mine once shared an assignment she'd give to her class to illustrate the persuasive power of language. Like a lot of language arts teachers, she'd heard plenty of gripes from her students about how "maybe the curtains were just blue" and "ugh, it's not that deep" when she asked them to analyze the language in a literary passage. She wanted to help them understand that the word choice in any piece of writing—literary, journalistic, even a social media post—goes beyond just reporting facts and can in fact change depending on context and aim.

The exercise worked like this: She'd ask the students to imagine that they'd been late to school that day for some made-up but realistic reason (overslept their alarm, missed the bus, ran out of gas, etc.) and write out how they'd explain what happened to their homeroom teacher—just a few sentences. Then she had them change it up: same situation, same reason for being late, but this time you're explaining it to your best friend. Then again, but *now* you're explaining it to your *crush*. And finally, now you're explaining it to an FBI agent.

Reading the four versions of the story aloud always got some good laughs and got her point across nicely. Whether we realize it or not, we change the way we speak depending on our relationship to the other person and what we want them to feel, think, or do as a result of what we tell them.

This is why, when you're doing any kind of self-talk, it's *so* important to draw on your Inner Bestie. Your Inner Bestie is what it sounds like: the part of yourself that's supportive, empathetic, encouraging, and understanding—just like a best friend. If you wouldn't say it to your best friend, then your Inner Bestie wouldn't say it to you.

The opposite of the Inner Bestie is the Inner Bully. This is the part of yourself that defaults to criticism, blame, or outright contempt, saying mean things intended to hurt and damage.

We all have *both* an Inner Bestie and an Inner Bully, but—just as in the creative writing exercise—we get to choose which of them we "speak" through when we talk to ourselves.

Think about it: When you're having that internal conversation about your day, your mistakes, or your challenges, which version of yourself are you channeling? Are you the FBI agent, interrogating yourself about every misstep and demanding an explanation? Is this your Inner Bully talking, or are you that best friend—the one who listens with compassion, offers perspective, and reminds you that everyone has rough days?

Most of us default to being our own harshest critic, to letting our Inner Bully have the mic, including and *especially* with our language—sometimes using words we'd never dream of using with a student or a colleague, let alone one who was struggling. But when we become aware of this pattern, we can make a different choice.

Mini-Experiment: Get out a pen and paper and write down what you would say to a friend if . . .

they were doing everything they could, but still felt as if they weren't doing enough.

they were doubting themselves when wanting to try something new that was really important to them.

they were exhausted but felt guilty about resting.

they made a mistake at work and couldn't stop thinking about it.

Notice what you wrote and how it sounds. Is it compassionate, understanding, encouraging? Is it humorous, upbeat, and generous? What energy are you bringing to your friend in this hypothetical situation?

Now repeat the exercise, but write down what you'd tell *yourself* in each of these scenarios. Take a look at the answers. What is the energy coming out? What's the tone, the overall argument? And, most important, who's talking? Is it your Inner Bestie, close to the way you'd talk to your *actual* bestie? Or is it your Inner Bully?

If your Inner Bully is speaking up, that's completely normal. Like all bullies, your Inner Bully just wants some attention. On a separate piece of paper, write out all your Inner Bully dialogue on the left side of the sheet. Really let it flow! Now *regulate your nervous system* and get in touch with your Inner Bestie. What do they say? Write all of *that* on the right side of the sheet.

What do you notice about the language you use? How do the words change? How does your body feel when you read what's on the left side versus what's on the right? Now you get to choose the one you want to have the mic.

For a PDF of the Inner Bestie/Inner Bully exercise, go to *empowerededucator.com/book.*

FIND AND REPLACE: CHANGE YOUR WORDS, CHANGE YOUR THINKING

Language is really one of my favorite topics to discuss, and not just because of all the incredible subtle yet powerful ways it's been proven to affect us as humans (or because I'm a card-carrying word nerd).

I love talking about language because language is what helps make understanding happen. It helps us demystify what's going on in our hearts and minds and give shape to what's inside us. It frames what we need to do so we can show up the way we want and align with *what* we want. Your language both directs *and* reflects where you're placing your attention.

This is why we need to be mindful *and* intentional about the words that come out of our mouths (or from our keyboards).

Now, that might sound like a *lot* of pressure, like you're going to have to be the language police on yourself, running every single noun and verb and adjective through a checkpoint before it gets all the way through—and causing a traffic jam in the process.

Fortunately, it's a lot simpler than that. Once we understand the words that hold the most power, that have the most influence over what we think and how we think it, we can swap words in and out quickly and easily, without others noticing: less *language police*, more *word ninja*.

Permanent and Pervasive or Spacious and Flexible

You've probably heard your fair share of *permanent, pervasive,* and *personal* language—especially if your students are on the younger side.

She ALWAYS gets picked for line leader! (There's a regular rotation.)

We haven't had recess in FOREVER. (It's been raining for two days in a row.)

I'm NEVER going to get this right. (They're *so* close . . . and just need to keep trying.)

Why are you picking on ME? (Everyone has to wash their hands, not just you, friend!)

We instinctively know that when kids use these big, sweeping words, they're not being accurate—they're just expressing big feelings. They're *reflecting* what's going on inside them, and as teachers, we help them *direct* (or *redirect*) their attention by helping them find different words.

But how often do we do the same for ourselves?

Psychologist Martin E. P. Seligman's theory of explanatory style proposes that human beings evaluate what happens to us on three axes: permanent, pervasive, and personal. In other words, we tend to interpret events in terms of *how long they'll last* (on a scale from *forever* to *a blip in time*), *how much of our lives they affect* (on a scale from *absolutely everything* to *a distinct, discrete area*), and *how much we had to do with causing them* (on a scale from *100 percent my fault* to *100 percent because of external factors*). Research has found that the more people characterize the events in their life as permanent, pervasive, and personal—that is, the more they see events as *forever, everywhere,* and *all my fault*—the more likely they are to experience depression and a sense of helplessness.

We might not realize it, but when we use permanent, pervasive, and personalized language—including words like *always*, *never*, *nothing*, and *every time*—we're limiting ourselves and constricting our ability to create, grow, or expand. And unlike our young students, no one's there to gently redirect us to think in terms that are more grounded . . . except, of course, ourselves.

In the abstract, it might seem obvious how these kinds of absolutist words can get in our way, and it may be hard to imagine where we ourselves might be using them (especially since we're probably not in a tantrum-throwing stage of life, where every big feeling we have gets verbalized aloud).

But consider these kinds of automatic thoughts you might have:

I'm never a morning person.

She's always late to faculty meetings.

Everything is really stressful.

I have the worst luck of anyone I know.

PERMANENT AND PERVASIVE LANGUAGE	EASY REPLACEMENTS
THESE WORDS ARE LIMITING:	**THESE WORDS ARE MORE ACCURATE AND EXPANSIVE:**
Always	Sometimes
Forever	Once in a while
All the time	Generally
Never	Often
Nothing	Frequently
Without exception	Repeatedly
Every time	Occasionally
Everything	Some things
Ever	Most of the time
	Right now/for now

Now, see what happens if you replace those words in the prior examples with expansive ones like *sometimes*, *occasionally*, or *some things*:

Sometimes I'm not a morning person.

She's *occasionally* late to faculty meetings.

Some things are really stressful *right now.*

I have *some* bad luck. So does everyone.

Can you feel how this is different? (And I mean really feel it in your body.)

Remember, your mind will always do what it thinks you want it to do—so stop asking it for what you don't want! If you're thinking and saying, "I never have enough time for myself," your language reflects where you're focusing your attention and directs you to more evidence of all the ways you never have time for yourself.

But if you say, "I sometimes don't have time for myself," or even "I frequently don't have time for myself," your focus is shifted slightly. Without being so constricted by *never*, your brain can peer into the divide you've created: *Sometimes* you don't have time, but other times, you do. What's different about those two kinds of situations? What might be causing the difference there? What actions could you take to shift the balance even further?

To be clear, swapping out permanent and pervasive language isn't some kind of magic wand, a "speak and make it so" kind of thing. (That's about as effective as Jerry Stiller demanding, "Serenity now!" on *Seinfeld* . . . although I may be dating myself with that reference. And if you haven't seen *Seinfeld,* do yourself a favor and watch that episode!) You're not outright *lying* about the way things are or even putting on rose-colored glasses; you're simply inviting your brain to be curious. Using more flexible and spacious language, we can still get our point across and give ourselves space to grow.

Can't vs. Won't

This word ninja swap almost feels *too* simple—or so I've been told.

"At first I was like . . . *can't* and *won't*? Aren't those basically explaining the same thing?" a teacher, Maria, once told me during one of my workshops. "But then I started to think through my own life and . . . yeah. There's just something much more powerful in saying *I won't be doing that*. I feel like a boss!"

Can't is a common word in our personal dialogue. How often do we say, "I can't do this" or "I can't do that"? *I can't join another committee. I can't drive the kids after school. I can't make dinner.*

The problem is that when we say "can't," we're abdicating our power. We're stating, basically, that we are physically incapable of doing something—that we have no choice in the matter. Yet for almost every single scenario in which we use *can't* on a regular basis, that's simply not true.

I can't join another committee. Sure you can . . . if you give up another chunk of what precious little free time you have.

I can't drive the kids after school. Sure you can . . . if you skip all the grading you need to do.

I can't make dinner. Sure you can . . . if you proceed to pull an all-nighter to finish your lesson plan.

Do you see what I mean? *I can't join another committee* isn't a statement of fact like *I can't fly* or *I can't breathe underwater* is . . . but when we say it that way, we trap ourselves into thinking that it is.

However, when we use *won't* instead, things change. We're acknowledging that we're *capable* of doing this thing, but we're *choosing* not to. It's empowering.

This is what Maria realized when she rewrote some of her own *can't*s into *won't*s.

In her case, she'd been asked to head up an after-school club. When she shifted from *I can't lead that club* to *I won't lead that club,* she started asking herself, "Okay, why won't I?" In her case, she felt like she didn't have enough time for herself after school was over, especially with kids of her own to go home to. That was interesting—and helped her feel empowered enough to say no.

Sometimes using *won't* gets you even deeper and creates more curiosity. For example, if you change from *I can't go to the retirement party* to *I won't go to the retirement party,* you'll ask yourself: *Okay, why won't I go?* Maybe you don't know many people there, and you're nervous about having no one to talk to because . . . *I can't talk to strangers.* Aha—but *can't* you? Maybe you try on *I won't talk to strangers* and realize that no, actually, you're willing to strike up a few conversations and see what happens. Basically, you start to question things and figure out if it's your own thoughts preventing you from going or if you really don't want to go.

This swap might feel uncomfortable at first. A lot of people find that *won't* feels surprisingly . . . rude, almost, and they're tempted to use *can't* because it feels more palatable and softer. If that's you, I hear you—and I encourage you to stay curious about it. Start with your internal dialogue: Acknowledging your *won't* on the inside, to yourself, is a great first step.

Changing *can't* into *won't* is one of the simplest but most powerful ways to get yourself thinking about the choices you're making. It helps you start to speak in the words of your future self, who feels the way they want to feel, has relationships with the people they want to, and gets the most out of life.

LET ME REPHRASE THAT

During my second year of teaching, I was directing *Cinderella Jr.* at my middle school, and I was *determined* to make it magical.

When I couldn't figure out how to create a convincing pumpkin carriage, I turned to this brand-new website called Craigslist (I know, I'm dating myself again . . .). Believe it or not, there was this gorgeous Cinderella carriage for sale from a school district down in Delaware. It was exactly what I needed *and* within my budget . . . so I rented the largest Penske truck I could find, drove all the way from Central New York to the middle of Delaware, and hauled this amazing-looking carriage back to school.

I told the kids, "If you want to thank me, don't touch it. *Do not touch the carriage.*" And my students listened. They heard those words loud and clear. They were *incredibly* respectful of my precious Craigslist carriage, and nothing happened to it.

But during our dress rehearsal, we hit a snag. This was the big transformation scene—we had dry ice machines and quick lighting cues creating the whole magical picture—and the timing of the transition just wasn't working at all. I was fully in my head, seeing the big picture I wanted, and in my frustration I said something like, "This isn't working. This transition needs to be cleaner."

One of the students working backstage—one of our stagehands—looked at me and said, "This is so frustrating to us. We're doing the best we can."

It hit me that they needed more support than I was actually giving them. So I paused and said, "You're right. I'm really sorry. I need to do better and explain more clearly what I mean. I thought I was giving you what you needed, but I need to give you more . . . and different, too. Can we sit down and work this out together?"

So the seven of us sat down together and made a plan. We created a little standard operating procedure for who was doing what, and after that, the scene ran like clockwork.

Later, one of the parents told me that this was the first time some of these kids had ever heard an adult speak to them that way—really listen to them, ask what they needed, and have enough self-reflection to say, "What I'm saying isn't actually what I mean. Let me try that again."

We don't always get our words right the first time—not to ourselves, and certainly not out loud to others. But as teachers, we are so susceptible to letting our ego take hold and refusing to back down, even when our words are clearly not serving us the way we want them to. That was certainly the case for me in my *Cinderella Jr.* days. I was twenty-three or twenty-four and thought I knew everything . . . or at least I wanted everyone to *think* I knew everything.

That's why those moments of "let me try this again" matter. You're not just hitting CTRL + Z and wiping out what you said from everyone's memory. You're resetting your impact with new, more precise language, *and* you're admitting that you missed the mark the first time around. You are showing, live and in person, what it looks like to learn from an experience and course-correct in real time. You are demonstrating humility and respect to your students—because that's what they deserve. And frankly, that often has more impact than getting it right in the first place.

It can feel scary to think about admitting to a mistake in front of a class (again, especially if you're a young teacher like I was at the time, feeling barely older than a middle school student myself). But showing that humility and respect doesn't mean giving up your authority. After all, did my drama students take what I said and use it as an excuse to run wild, ignore any further instructions, and generally throw things into chaos? Not at all. In fact, what I did actually made them listen *even better,* because it showed that I was as invested in their success as they were—and more invested in ensuring we had a good show than I was in being right.

So the next time you find yourself wishing you could take your words back . . . go ahead and do just that.

EASY SCRIPTS FOR REPHRASING

"Hold on, that was poorly worded. Let me try again."

"Actually, let me rephrase that."

"Before we go on, I just want to come back to something I said a few minutes ago that's not sitting right. What I really meant to say was . . ."

CUT THE COMPLAINING AND STOP THE GOSSIP

Picture the typical faculty room at a school. Now tune into the conversations at the coffee machine, the photocopier, the seats and tables. What do you pick up?

You will not believe *what one student's mother emailed to me last night . . .*

. . . class is just out of control, never been so disrespected in my life . . .

. . . and there's no budget to pay for it, as usual . . .

. . . eating up all my planning periods, like I have just hours *to spare . . .*

Now that we understand how language and the reticular activating system work together, we know that complaining or gossiping literally tells our brain we want to feel bad. It shows us more evidence of how to feel bad. It keeps us dwelling in negativity.

We understand how it works and why it's something to avoid. We understand that we don't have to engage in that anymore.

And yet . . . we still do it.

Let's be real: gossiping, venting, and complaining are hard habits to break. Gossiping about others is almost primal human behavior: It's how we establish our personal reputation in a group and define and refine social norms, among other things.[7] (It's why we love shows like *Bridgerton* or get excited to spread the news when a friend gets engaged or has a baby.) But gossip can also make people feel less psychologically safe,[8] less cooperative,[9] and more fearful and self-conscious.[10]

These benefits can be particularly appealing to us as teachers. We work in highly social, hierarchical environments. In school systems, information is power, and belonging to the in-group can feel essential for survival. We bond over shared frustrations about difficult students, unreasonable parents, or administrative decisions that seem to come from another planet. Gossip can be a way for us to process the emotional labor of our jobs and feel less alone in our struggles.

But that doesn't erase the harmful effects, like eroding trust within our school communities, creating an atmosphere of fear, and speaking the very negativity and stress we're trying to escape into existence. Gossiping and complaining are low-level behaviors that don't move us forward toward the person we want to be. They're continuing to perpetuate all these negative narratives and keep us swimming in that emotional sludge when we know better now. So I'm going to ask you to try something: signing a No Complaining/Gossiping Agreement.

Exercise: No Complaining/Gossiping Agreement

Write or type this out and sign it at the bottom. This is your commitment to yourself (and your future self). You can also grab a printable copy on my website at *empowerededucator .com/book*.

> I, [YOUR NAME], hereby declare that I will not gossip or complain for seven consecutive days. I am making this commitment to align with my thoughts and actions to become a better version of myself. My words are powerful, and they reflect and direct my focus and attention. I will no longer engage in complaints and gossip. Engaging in complaining and gossiping is disempowering, and it no longer serves me.

Consider it another experiment—you're not bound to this forever and ever, but for the period you commit to it, follow it steadfastly.

When I present this No Complaining/Gossiping Agreement to teachers, I usually receive one of two comments. The first is, "But, Jen, this is how I connect with people! We sit together at lunch and chat about all the latest drama at the school—it's how we bond."

To that, I say, "Yep, your relationships are probably going to change. That specific behavior isn't in line with your commitment, is it?"

And . . . what a beautiful opportunity to address it head on. If someone launches into an "Ooh, did you hear . . ." you can step up and say, "Hey, I'm actually participating in a no complaining, no gossiping experiment. I'm not going to be able to have this conversation. Can we talk about something else?"

If there's some pushback, you've got some choices. For example, "Listen, I would love it if you could support me in my experiment. It's actually really interesting—do you want to know more about it?" (A little subject change *and* a chance to get more people on board!)

If the pushback persists, and it's clear that your colleagues aren't going to respect a boundary you've set, well, here's an opportunity to make a different choice about how you spend your lunch break. That's the thing about boundaries (which we'll dive into more in the next chapter): When you begin to change and elevate and grow, your relationships might grow and evolve with you, or they might not. Both of those things are perfectly okay.

The second response I often get is: "But, Jen, you said no complaining, but what about venting? Isn't venting healthy? I thought it was important to process our emotions, after all."

To *that,* I say, Absolutely! You need to process your emotions. But that doesn't *have* to mean venting.

First off, feelings happen in your body. So if you feel like you need to release something, get that body moving. Go for a run, hit a punching bag, swing by a rage room and smash some plates, scream in your car, get a medicine ball and throw it down a couple of times—whatever you need to do physically to move that emotional energy.

Second, remember, all emotions are valid, even the ones that don't feel good—which is why you need to take proactive steps to process them. But when we're venting, we're not really *processing.* We might "get something off our chest," but it doesn't disappear—it just gets, well, off our chest. In other words, often just giving ourselves space and time to say the things that are on our minds—that is to say, venting—*without actually processing the emotion* is perpetuating the problem, recycling it ad nauseam.

The fact is, venting and complaining are cousins. This is an invitation to be cognizant about what's coming out of your mouth all the time.

If you want to get everything out verbally, that's normal and can be really helpful. Sometimes we just need to be unfiltered and unpolished in our speech and process through our words. What matters is who we're sharing our thoughts with and making sure it's intentional. Trusted friends, mentors, and colleagues are the ones who can serve as a kind of container and sounding board for what we need to express. Less optimal audiences are the people who will just take what we say and use it as fuel for the rumor mill. Having a conversation with intention means going in knowing what you're trying to achieve: processing something out loud into a sympathetic ear, sharing and seeking advice, venting to a safe person in a safe space to embody the emotions that come up. Without that intention, you start to fall into the space of complaining.

The other piece I want to be clear about is this: Give yourself grace. We are human, and when you catch yourself complaining, gossiping, or venting in a way that feels like crap, those are beautiful moments of awareness for you to regulate your nervous system, get curious about it, and give it another try.

So while I've given you a contract, I also want to acknowledge that it's not one and done. Recommitment is *always* a thing—emphasis on *always*. (Yes, I really mean it here!) It is an expected part of life. You are going to be committing and recommitting to yourself. To your vision. To that amazing next-level version of you who feels unshakable, whose nervous system is cool, calm, relaxed, and resilient as you move through your life.

Expect to fall off the bandwagon, and you can feel excited to get back on.

MAIN TAKEAWAYS

- Words can trigger physical responses in your brain and body, and the language you use directs your brain's attention through the reticular activating system.
- Replacing permanent and pervasive language like *always/never* and *can't* with empowered, flexible language like *sometimes* and *won't* creates a sense of agency for yourself.
- When in doubt, speak to yourself with the same compassion you'd show a friend, and give your Inner Bully the attention it's requiring.
- Complaining and gossiping are as human as it gets, but these behaviors can program your brain to focus on problems rather than solutions. Committing *not* to gossip or complain is a powerful way to shift your context (and you can download your own contract to print and sign at *empowerededucator.com/book*).

8

EXPERIENCE WELLNESS THAT LASTS

A few years ago, my son, Ethan, was out sick from school. Nothing serious, just one of those typical childhood bugs that requires rest and recovery. My intuition told me it'd be at least a two-day absence, so later that evening after his first day home sick, I sent a quick message through the school app to his teacher: "Hey, looks like Ethan is going to be out tomorrow, too—just wanted to check in about his schoolwork so he can catch back up when he's healthy. Thanks!"

I sent the message then because, well, that's when I had a spare minute to get to it. I was *not* expecting a reply anytime soon. But at nine o'clock that same evening—yes, nine p.m.—my phone rang. It was Ethan's teacher, apologizing for the late hour because of her hectic evening putting her kids to bed, calling to see how he was feeling (still feverish, alas), and making sure he had everything he needed for his assignments.

As a parent, I was touched by her thoughtfulness. She clearly cared about my sick kiddo, *and* she wanted to reassure me that he'd be able to keep up on schoolwork. But as a fellow teacher, my heart ached a bit for her. This was her evening, too, after all. When was *she* getting time to take care of *herself*?

To be clear, she did nothing *wrong*, and I am not judging or criticizing her. Her actions were borne out of a deep sense of caring and responsibility, which is admirable. But what that late-night call really demonstrated to me is that she was falling into the same rut that I fell into along with so many teachers: the tendency to put everyone *else's* well-being before our own, *often to our own detriment*. That's not just unsustainable; it's completely backward.

On a certain level, we all know we need to take care of ourselves in order to do our best work. It's the oxygen-mask principle again: Put yours on first *before* helping others (because if you pass out from lack of air, that helps *no one* . . . least of all you!).

In practice, though, we will almost *always* put others before ourselves. My son's teacher felt that no matter what time of night it was, she couldn't take time for herself—whatever that might have meant for her—until she had ensured that a sick child could catch up on his work when he returned to school. Like so many of us, she emotionally pretzeled herself for everyone else's comfort, assuming that to prove her worth, to show she is doing everything right, to take care of others the *right* way, she had to sacrifice her own needs in some way.

No wonder our well-being is so . . . well, *un*well. Our self-sacrifice, our emotional pretzeling, and what Terri Cole calls our "high-functioning codependency" with our work is taking a toll on not just our minds, but our bodies as well—sometimes in frightening ways (remember the teacher with the kidney stones from not drinking enough water?).[1]

Educators are used to sacrificing their well-being for the

greater good of their students, their family, and the community. We're caught in this endless loop of giving, helping, and nurturing without nourishing ourselves enough to relieve the stress of our demanding jobs. Surveys have found that K-12 teachers are the most burnt-out profession in the United States.[2] Studies about the impact of the pandemic on work-related stress even found that teachers in the U.S. are 40 percent more likely to have anxiety and depression in comparison with frontline healthcare workers.[3]

These statistics are alarming and prove that educators need real solutions that will help us take better care of ourselves. Surface level "self-care" like face masks and mani-pedis aren't going to do the trick. The extra-large, extra-caf pick-me-ups that so many of us love aren't going to help in the long term, either. Our doctors notice we're running ourselves ragged and tell us we need to reduce our stress, but don't have any suggestions for *how* we might do that. Even a luxurious getaway can feel like a Band-Aid fix that instead is more like a weeklong case of the Sunday Scaries, leaving you unable to relax because you're so stressed over all the things you *aren't* getting done.

The good news is, well-being is possible for teachers and is actually quite simple at its core. We *can* go above and beyond for our students, but only when we take care of our own needs first. That's the difference between burning out and sustaining ourselves.

Now that you've articulated your mission and vision, learned more about metacognition and language, and seen how the practices of reflection and advocacy help you feel more empowered through small, regular action, you know that well-being isn't a one-off. Well-being is an *active* way of being (*being* is right in the word), and it requires the application and embodiment of everything you've learned so far in this book. With all that under your belt, you have what you need to engage with your well-being truly, fully, and sustainably—to feel better in the day-to-day, so you can do better *every* day.

REDEFINING WELL-BEING

Well-being is a verb, not a noun. It's something we *do,* something we *live out*. The problem is, we don't think of it that way. Instead, we think of well-being as something we have (or don't have). This inevitably leads to shame when we're "not hitting the mark" (because no one hits the mark 100 percent of the time), and that shame in turn discourages us from pursuing well-being further.

So let's redefine the term. Instead of a binary state or a have-it-or-don't quality, think of *well-being* as consistent intention and purposeful attention toward your holistic hygiene. Like physical hygiene, it requires daily attention to all aspects of yourself. And also like physical hygiene, it's a constant work in progress: The same way you can't take one ten-hour shower and expect to be clean for the rest of your life, or book one marathon dentist appointment and never touch a toothbrush again, you can't one-and-done your well-being. Rather, it's small, consistent actions (just like you do to maintain your physical hygiene) that will keep you in the best shape possible.

That said, well-being isn't about surface-level self-care. As a buzzword, *self-care* has become synonymous with quick fixes and indulgences like spa days, bubble baths, and mini shopping sprees, but that's not how it started out. The term is partially rooted in the civil rights and feminist movements (and in their mission to uplift communities who could not afford or were excluded from many self-preserving wellness practices and services) and partially in the medical field, referring to basic survival capabilities of tending to eating, dressing, bathing, and so on that are necessary steps to full recovery from a health setback. In pop culture and some of the wellness industry, self-care also has a tendency to reinforce the very problem it's trying to solve: that you need to *earn* rest, that things that make you feel good are a *treat* or an *indulgence* that come only *after* you've run your tank down to empty.

Well-being, on the other hand, makes those acts of caring for yourself a given—no matter *what* the external situation is like. If self-care is like cramming for a test the night before, well-being is like studying consistently throughout the semester. You're building a solid foundation that you can rely on in acute moments of stress (like an exam). Regardless of what happens, you have a reserve of holistic strength and agency to draw on in how you react.

Well-being is also not precisely the same thing as another concept that often crops up in this arena: *resilience*. Resilience is another popular term for what we supposedly should be striving for as teachers . . . but in my mind, it's a bit flawed. In fact, I used to resent the word *resilience*. I remember one time my therapist said to me, "Jen, you're probably the most resilient person I know." At that moment, I knew she meant it as a compliment. But I left that session feeling angry. I didn't want to be resilient—I wanted the shitstorm to stop!

The problem originates in the roots of the word itself. *Resilience* literally means to "jump back into place" . . . but sometimes we don't actually *need* to return to the status quo. In fact, trying to return to where we were before can be harmful when it promotes any bypass of the real issues we're facing.

That's why I now prefer to think of resilience as a *flexible mind*—the ability to thrive regardless of circumstances. When we try to force ourselves back to some previous state, we create a mismatch between our inner and outer worlds. But when we allow ourselves to be flexible, to adapt and grow through our experiences, we're not just surviving—we're thriving in whatever circumstances life presents us with. We are *adapting* to the new reality. So true resilience isn't just about bouncing back to where you were before or stopping in your tracks. It's about recognizing that when the outer environment changes, you must navigate your inner environment as well, because that's how you keep moving forward.

WHY TEACHERS STRUGGLE WITH WELL-BEING

The reason I'm spending so much time defining well-being and resilience isn't just academic (although I do love my etymology). It's because teachers face some unique challenges when it comes to actually practicing it. So now it's time to examine the other half of the equation: what makes it so easy for us to feel stuck in a place of burnout.

As teachers, we have a tendency to get caught in what's called the *cycle of sacrifice and renewal,* a term coined by Annie McKee and Richard E. Boyatzis in their book *Resonant Leadership.*[4] This is the pattern where we give endlessly to others (sacrifice phase) until we're completely depleted, then attempt unsustainable quick fixes like bubble baths or mental health days (renewal phase). But since these surface-level solutions don't address the root cause, we immediately return to sacrificing on empty, drawing on resources we've already tapped out. As a result, most teachers find themselves perpetually in the sacrifice phase, never reaching true renewal.

What makes us so uniquely susceptible to this cycle? It's not that we're just naturally giving people (although many—if not most—of us are). It's that we've developed a unique kind of codependent relationship with our work. As I mentioned earlier, this is what psychotherapist and relationship expert Terri Cole calls *high-functioning codependency*. Unlike the traditional concept of a codependent person (typically someone who enables the unhealthy or addictive behaviors of others), those with high-functioning codependent tendencies (often highly capable and accomplished people) are overinvested in the feelings, needs, and problems of others, to the point of neglecting their own needs. High-functioning codependency is why we ignore or minimize our own problems but jump in feetfirst to solve problems for others—or even just to keep them happy and comfortable. We derive our sense of worth from how well we tend to others, regardless of whether we run ourselves ragged in the process.

Unfortunately (but unsurprisingly), this codependent relationship with our work—and with our students—works against us. For one thing, we're so focused on the well-being of other people that we neglect our own. We make phone calls at nine p.m. when we desperately need sleep (or just some time to *not be working*), or we hold off on *drinking water* because we don't feel we can spare three minutes for a bathroom break. This is especially insidious if you identify with the trifecta of being a mom, a woman, and a teacher—those roles come with multiple layers of conditioning that tell you to put everyone else's needs first. (Men have their own conditioning, absolutely, but the intersection of these three identities creates a perfect storm of self-sacrifice.)

For another thing, relying on other people's approval is especially damaging to our well-being as teachers because of who the other people around us tend to be—kids. When we're operating from a place of high-functioning codependency, we're handing our self-worth over to children whose brains aren't even fully formed yet. So it makes sense that we're going to take it personally when some kid tells us off. But the truth is, that interaction has nothing to do with us. To quote the amazing Dr. Becky Kennedy, the kid isn't giving us a hard time; the kid is *having* a hard time. When we look to them for praise, approval, or any validation of our self-worth, we're expecting something from them that isn't always accurate, fair, reasonable, or their place to give, and that only reinforces our sense of burnout.

Moreover, our fellow adults aren't equipped for the task of validating our self-worth, nor do they need to be. The colleagues and administrators we see every day, the parents and school board members we work closely with—all of them are contending with their own internal (and external) realities. Their emotional state isn't something we can ever fully know for sure, let alone influence or control—so to stake our well-being on it is to live in constant uncertainty at best.

All of this culminates in the When-Then Cycle: the idea that we'll finally feel the way we want to feel when—and only when—something external changes. Do any of these statements sound familiar?

When I get tenure, then I'll finally feel secure.

When my students' test scores improve, then I'll finally feel successful.

When the school administrators appreciate me, then I'll finally feel valued.

When my students behave better, then I'll finally feel confident.

When parents stop complaining, then I'll finally feel respected.

The When-Then Cycle is seductive because it makes it *feel* like we're aiming for some bigger goal of how we want to feel, but in reality we're just handing over the remote control to external forces we can't influence, let alone control.

Think about what happens on any given school day. You walk into the building feeling pretty good, but then your principal doesn't make eye contact when you pass in the hallway. Suddenly your internal monologue spirals: *Did I do something wrong? Are they mad at me? Maybe I said something and she took it the wrong way. I'm always so awkward.* Your whole emotional state crashes based on someone else's facial expression—which, for all you know, had nothing to do with you and everything to do with their own overwhelming inbox. Then you get to your classroom and a student says, "I love this class!" after your lesson. Your mood lifts! You feel competent again—valued and like you've done enough. Except, wait . . . lunch rolls around, and a colleague makes an offhand comment about your "unusual" bulletin-board display, and your mood plummets once more.

This emotional ping-pong is exhausting, and it's keeping you from the sustained sense of fulfillment and joy that creates a healthy longevity in this career. When we live in the When-Then Cycle, we're constantly scanning our environment for evidence of our worth, our competence, our value—and inevitably coming up short, because external validation is both unpredictable and ultimately unsatisfying.

The antidote to this cycle starts with fundamentally redefining what success means to you. For most of us, our definition of success was shaped by decades in the very school system we now work in—a system that taught us that success looks like gold stars, good grades, and perfect attendance awards. We learned to measure our worth by applause, accolades, and external approval. When that's added to our evolutionary need for social acceptance, it's no wonder that we fall into the conditional happiness trap so easily.

True success, however, doesn't have to be about what other people think of your performance. It can be about how aligned *you* feel with yourself at the end of each day. And that is something you can stay curious about, take action toward, and *own*, fully and completely.

Exercise: Reframing Success

Instead of asking yourself "Did I do enough?" or "Did I get enough positive feedback today?" try asking these questions:

- How did I feel today?
- Did I say what needed to be said?
- Did I show up authentically for my students?
- Am I living in alignment with my core values?
- Do I like the person I see in the mirror?

Instead of letting external factors dictate your sense of self-worth and happiness, come up with your own definition of success, and look curiously and nonjudgmentally at how well you're achieving it. It can be a game changer—truly.

Recently, I was working with a school district for the day, teaching them some of these strategies, and afterward, a school nurse came up, eager to talk to me. She shared that these ideas really resonated with her because of what she'd experienced when the going got especially tough during the pandemic. As a nurse, she was on what felt like every front line at once, and the worry over how well she was doing every day was eating away at her. Until one day, she made a conscious change: Rather than worrying about whether she did enough on any given day, she started to ask herself simply: *How did I make a difference today?*

That shift changed everything for her. With that one simple question, she could see so clearly that her work every day had a positive impact, and she weathered the roughest months of that school year with an inner sense of well-being. To this day, she's thriving in what she does and feels hugely successful—because she *is* making a difference, every single day. (And so are you.)

DO SOME CPR: RECLAIM YOUR AGENCY WITH COMPLETE PERSONAL RESPONSIBILITY

Now that we understand what well-being truly *is* and why we tend to fall into traps of external validation, it's time to seize some empowerment. There's a simple well-being practice that can start to rewire our emotional default from the When-Then Cycle and its reliance on external factors to a state of proactive, conscious agency: Complete Personal Responsibility, or CPR—because yes, it really is that lifesaving.

Complete Personal Responsibility is about recognizing that while you can't control what happens around you, you do have complete agency over how you respond to it. For example, you might have an initial reaction when your principal announces yet another new initiative during your planning period or when a parent sends a passive-aggressive email questioning your teaching methods. That's human. But you get to choose what happens next. You can let that moment define your entire day, spiraling through frustration and resentment, or you can acknowledge the feeling, process it as you need to, and decide how you want to show up from that point forward, using the tools that you've learned so far in this book. That's CPR in action—and *that's* looking after your own well-being.

The first step in taking CPR is getting honest about how you actually feel throughout your day, and that means paying attention to the signals coming from your body (as we learned in chapter 1). It's so easy to keep your head down, your eyes on the road, and just *go go go* through the day while bottling up or suppressing any emotions as they spring up. Opening an emotional door can feel like opening the floodgates (sometimes literally, if crying is how your emotions tend to come out). That's so real and valid. But what's equally real is the second part of CPR: knowing that all feelings serve a purpose and listening to what they're telling you.

Experiment:
Tracking Your Emotional State

As you move through a typical school day—from the time you wake up through your commute and your interactions with students and colleagues, right up until you go to bed—track your emotional state once every hour. You can do this however you'd like, from notes on your phone to jotting in your planner or even a full-on sticker chart (I see you, elementary school teachers!), but it's important that you have some kind of record you can reflect on. (You can also download a premade tracker from my resources page at *empowerededucator.com/book.*)

Once you've done this tracking experiment, look at what you've recorded. How much of your day are you spending in *empowering* feelings versus *disempowering* ones? Try it for a few days in a row or a few days a week so you can look for patterns.

> *Examples of empowering feelings:* love, gratitude, hope, joy, pride, inspiration, courage, ease, confidence, motivation, peace
>
> *Examples of disempowering feelings:* doubt, insecurity, sadness, hopelessness, anxiety, shame, anger, worry, overwhelm, frustration, loneliness, guilt

This experiment can be eye-opening. Once you start tracking how you feel during the course of a day, you might be surprised by how much time you spend in those disempowering states. Many educators discover they've been running on emotional fumes without even realizing it. One teacher, after completing this audit, admitted that she had a hard time getting through a single day without tears of one kind or another. She'd just never taken the time to get curious about the kind of disempowering emotions that might be in play.

You might also realize that you've been waiting for external circumstances to change before you allow yourself to feel good. Another teacher observed that her emotional state shifted dramatically based on her environment: "It's so easy for me to feel empowering feelings when I'm at home and surrounded by support, but then I get to school and it's like a switch flips: boom, disempowering." *Yes*. This is the When-Then Cycle in action again, but this time tied to *where* we are, and it's particularly common in school settings, where so much feels outside our control.

But here's where taking Complete Personal Responsibility changes things. Instead of waiting for permission to feel the way you want to or letting circumstances "make" you feel a certain way, you get to own how you're feeling. You have far more agency over your emotional experience than you might have believed. Instead of emotionally outsourcing through unhelpful or even self-sabotaging coping methods, take the last step of CPR—moving toward a proactive, intentional approach toward your emotional well-being.

If the When-Then Cycle operates on "When X happens, I can finally feel [insert empowering feeling]," then this is the opposite: "I want to be feeling Y, so what aligned actions can I take?" For example, if you decide you want to feel at ease, and some external event threatens that feeling (e.g., a colleague doesn't say hello in the hallway—cue the panicked "Is he mad at me?!" downward spiral), you can pause, ask yourself *What do I need to do right now to feel more at ease?* and choose an action that realigns you with your desired state, such as regulating your nervous system, going through the Fact or Fiction? exercise (from chapter 4), taking a walk, or doing some stretching to move your body in space.

According to neuroscientist Dr. Jill Bolte Taylor, the chemical rush that creates a feeling lasts only about ninety seconds.[5] A minute and a half! That's it! What's wild is that the feeling *can* last longer than that, but only if you continue thinking the same thought that triggered it. No emotion is final—and what's more, we can choose to work through it and shift it.

That's not to say we're going to bypass what we're feeling, trying to fast-forward it all so that we can get to the next state of being. Part of CPR is honoring our feelings, processing them, and releasing them (which is especially critical if we want to avoid them manifesting as physical symptoms like high blood pressure or back pain). A metaphor I find really useful for this process comes from authors and researchers (and sisters!) Emily and Amelia Nagoski. In their brilliant book *Burnout*, they describe emotions as tunnels, something you can move through and eventually come out the other end of, *if* you keep moving.[6] It might take you a little bit longer to get through some tunnels than others, but what matters is recognizing that every emotion *is* something you can get through—not a pit you're falling into and never escaping.

This shift in perspective isn't just powerful for you—it's transformative for your students, too. As one teacher, Rehka, shared in a workshop, "My students' favorite phrase might be 'Miss Rehka, he or she made me mad!' Now I can explain to them that yes, the other student is responsible for controlling him or herself, and this doesn't excuse any of those actions, but you also have a choice in how you respond and what you want to feel. It's okay to feel mad, just know that how long you stay mad is your choice. It's pretty groundbreaking for them . . . and for me!"

When you model this kind of emotional ownership for your students, you're teaching them one of life's most valuable skills. But taking complete personal responsibility for your emotions is only half the equation. The other half is learning to protect and preserve your emotional well-being through clear, consistent boundaries—which is exactly what we're going to explore next.

THE IMPORTANCE OF BOUNDARIES

Early in my career, I was fortunate to have the mentorship of an amazing veteran teacher. Her name was Penny, and she was a *gem*. A more seasoned middle school band teacher, Penny had been teaching for decades and had clearly gotten to that point in life when she stopped giving a shit what other people did and kept her eyes on her own paper.

For me, a new teacher who cared very *deeply* about what other people said, did, and thought of me, I found Penny's attitude of easy, quiet confidence fascinating. *How does that work?* I wondered. *What is that like? How can I be more like you?*

So I observed not just how Penny taught her students, but how she navigated everything. If a new policy had most teachers bent out of shape, railing and moaning against it, I'd see how Penny would hang back and contemplate. I'd practically see her wheels turning: *How do I show up to this thing? Am I going to invest my energy in it? Let it get a rise out of me? Or is it something I can take off my mental plate?* Then she'd act accordingly.

Penny showed me what it looked like to make intentional choices about where to put your energy—not just reacting to every new initiative or crisis that came down the pipeline, but actually deciding what deserved your attention and what didn't. She was putting her well-being first—dealing with her own oxygen mask before helping others. She had mastered something I didn't even know existed yet: the art of choosing your battles and protecting your peace in the process. The art, in short, of boundaries.

If your hackles got raised up at the mention of the B-word, you're not alone. Creating a boundary (or even thinking about creating one) can actually tap into a primal fear. Back when humans were hunting and gathering, being chased by predators and huddling together through ice storms, community was survival. If you were excommunicated, you were pretty much toast. Thus staying on everyone's good side—people-pleasing—was literally a survival strategy.

All of which is to say, if boundaries make you uncomfortable, there's nothing wrong with you. You are not broken. You're human and working as intended. Those people-pleasing tendencies exist for evolutionary reasons, and you're simply responding accordingly. (Not to mention that they've probably been reinforced over all the decades of your life.)

However, setting boundaries is critical for our well-being—a regular practice that allows us to reassert, day by day, even minute by minute, what we need and *don't* need. They're the best tool we have against high-functioning codependency.

A lot of the discomfort around boundaries comes from their somewhat fuzzy definition, so let's be clear on what boundaries actually are before we jump into setting any. In the popular imagination, boundaries are often characterized as a way of exerting control over others or as walls shutting people out. In reality, boundaries aren't about other people at all. Boundaries are actually about you.

Here's an example to illustrate what this means. Recently, I was folding all my kids' clothes, grumbling a bit (because it's my *least* favorite chore), when the thought struck me: Why the *hell* was I doing my kids' laundry for them? I'd always hated doing it, and they were now more than old enough to handle it themselves.

So I held a little family meeting and told my kids: "Listen up. From now on, I'm not doing your laundry anymore. That chore is now your responsibility. I will walk you through the process and show you how. You can do it or not, but I'm no longer available to do it for you."

That's a boundary. The action is mine. I'm not telling them what to do; I'm saying, "Here's what my action is going to be, and you can respond how you see fit."

Of course they bucked at this—at first. But I held firm, and once they realized Mom was really not going to be washing and drying and folding their stuff anymore, and it was either "do your own laundry or go to school in dirty clothes," they rose to the occasion . . . eventually.

That's not to say that boundaries are always that easily drawn—*but* I was also fully prepared to hold firm if they *didn't* start doing their own wash. I'd been through this already: Before announcing that the laundry itself was their responsibility, I'd actually laid down a similar boundary about picking up their clothes. I told them I was no longer available to keep their stuff off the floor, and if the T-shirts and socks nevertheless *stayed* on the floor, then I was going to take further action (in that case, no devices or TV until the chores got done). Again, I wasn't telling them what to do. They didn't *have* to pick up their clothes, but they knew full well that if they didn't, my next action was well-defined, and I was going to carry it out.

That's what boundaries actually are—they're about what *you're* going to do, not about controlling what other people do. And yes, this can feel very uncomfortable! For all those hardwired human reasons, laying out those boundaries doesn't often feel good at first—especially if you end up needing to follow through on that second action.

EXAMPLES OF BOUNDARIES

Not a boundary: The kids can't be in my room during lunch anymore.

Boundary: I will be shutting my door during lunch. If kids want to come in, I will give them an alternate time to meet with me.

Not a boundary: You can't talk to me that way—how dare you?!

Boundary: I'm not available to be spoken to that way. I'm happy to continue this conversation when we're both feeling a little bit more regulated.

Not a boundary: Parents, I will not allow you to email me during weekend hours.

Boundary: Parents, if you send an email after three p.m. on Friday, I will respond no sooner than Monday morning.

When you establish boundaries, you're almost certain to run into some pushback. The people who are going to buck at your boundary are also the same people who have benefited from your *not* having the boundary. When they push back, say your boundary again and follow through (or you escalate it to a meta-boundary about this very conversation: *I'm no longer available to continue discussing this. If you don't respect my boundary, I will . . .*). Someone barges in during your lunch wanting to discuss something? "Actually, I'm not available to chat right now, but I can talk at three p.m. Does that work for you?" They show up the next day, same time? "As I said before, I'm not available to talk during lunch. What other time works for you?" You can even state exactly what you're doing: "To be transparent, I'm setting a boundary here. Thank you for understanding."

This can feel hard—I know it does. We're not used to it, so it's not comfortable and doesn't feel safe (hello, amygdala!). But sticking to your boundaries is always worth it, because that's where your power lies. And just because you fail to stick to a boundary once doesn't mean you can't reassert it next time. This isn't a zero-sum game; you always have an opportunity to try again. (Also, it should be noted that this section is a starting point into a big topic: People can and have written entire books on boundaries, and I highly encourage you to explore further.)

In one of my workshops about boundaries, an administrator expressed his concern about lots of people suddenly having boundaries. "Wouldn't this mean that lots of people are going to say NO, with a bunch of teachers drawing lines in the sand? Everything would grind to a halt!" While I understand the fear, what really happens is quite the opposite. When people express their agency in making boundaries for themselves, they show up happier, more present, more engaged, and they say yes more willingly and genuinely to the things that truly align with their mission and vision (which can also align with the mission and vision of the school).

The best thing about boundaries is that even though they're about you and what *you're* available to do, they can also expand the idea of what's possible for other people. When you show that it's possible *not* to settle for the status quo, but to decide actively and consciously what you will and won't accept, it can create a ripple effect. Other teachers, or even students, can model their behavior on what they see you doing and how they see you thriving. That's how culture starts to shift within a school.

THE WELL-BEING SAVINGS ACCOUNT

Think of well-being like a savings account. Every small practice you do—whether it's taking three deep breaths between classes, celebrating a tiny win, or setting a boundary with a colleague—makes a deposit. Over time, these deposits accumulate, giving you reserves to draw from when the inevitable challenges hit. You're not constantly scrambling to find energy or calm in the moment you need it most and maxing out your emotional line of credit. Instead, you've got what you need all ready to go because you've been building it up bit by bit, day by day. That's what keeps you in the *renewal* stage of the cycle—and out of the depletion—for good.

What does that look like in practice? Here are some simple exercises that can help you build up that savings account, even if you're starting from scratch.

Exercise: Mindfulness

This could be as simple as those breathing breaks we've talked about throughout this book, or it could be yoga, prayer, meditation, or any practice that helps you stay centered and present. The key is acknowledging where you are right now—not where you think you should be, but where you actually are. Whether it's a short interval between classes to notice your breath or a few minutes of meditation before bed, these small moments of presence add up to create a foundation of calm you can access when you need it most. For guided meditations, go to *empowereducator.com/book*.

Exercise: Gratitude

I know gratitude practices can feel a little cliché, but stick with me here. When you're expressing gratitude, there's one simple trick that makes all the difference: Add the word *because* to your statements.

Instead of saying, "I'm grateful for my morning coffee," try "I'm grateful for my morning coffee because it gives me a few quiet minutes to myself before the day begins." That little word *because* attaches emotion to your gratitude and gives you all the benefits of this practice by connecting you to something bigger than just the surface-level acknowledgment. I'm grateful for my colleague because she always makes me laugh when I'm feeling stressed and reminds me not to take everything so seriously. I'm grateful for technology because it allows me to connect with people and resources from all around the world.

When you add that *because*, you're not just going through the motions—you're making a real connection. You might even get some "gratitears"—when you're so grateful for something that you start to well up. That's a beautiful way to process that emotion!

Exercise: Hope

Hope brings you to a place that's out of your current reality, and that's incredibly powerful for renewal. Use your imagination to get excited about something in the future—a vacation you're planning, a project you're working on, plans with friends, or even your weekend. You can also connect to your vision from chapter 3, imagining the teacher and person you're becoming. Hope is about giving yourself something positive to move toward. Hope generates excitement and energy that can carry you through tough days. And if you need some inspiration, remember that where flowers bloom, so does hope. Look there, too.

Exercise: Compassion and Self-Connection

This isn't about the type of compassion that leads to compassion fatigue—that constant giving and giving that drains us. This is about connection that fills you up. Think about walking your dog, calling a friend, having lunch with someone you care about, scheduling a date night (or what happens after date night!). These moments of genuine connection with someone or something that brings you fulfillment create a sense of renewal that goes way beyond just getting through your to-do list.

Exercise: Joy, Laughter, and Playfulness

At some point during the process of growing up, we all decided that as we got older, we needed to get serious and buckle down all the time. But incorporating daily joy, laughter, and playfulness into your life is incredibly powerful for your well-being.

For example, I recently heard about an adult tap-dancing class near me, and I thought, *How cool is that?* It's fun, it's joyful, it's playful, it's active, and it's something to look forward to every week. The same goes for my friend who just started taking fencing classes in her mid-thirties—she knows she's not going to make the Olympics, but she's having a blast, as she puts it, "playing around with swords." It's all about the sheer joy of the experience.

Maybe one of your students earnestly draws a portrait of you with wild purple hair "because I couldn't find a brown crayon." Maybe you spot a goofy bumper sticker on your way to work that makes you chuckle. Maybe your barista draws a smiley face next to your name on your cup. Maybe you decide to throw some Funfetti sprinkles in with your morning yogurt and granola just to make it pretty.

The point is: Do more of whatever brings you joy and laughter, and notice all the joy that pops up around you. Your inner child is still within you, and they want you to keep finding all the delightful things that are out in the world.

Exercise: Movement

One of the smartest purchases I've ever made came after a particularly awful night of insomnia. I was exhausted, my muscles were aching, and I was *mad* (because the sun was coming up and I hadn't slept a wink). I remember that I went downstairs to the living room, grabbed one of the pillows, and punched it a few times . . . and maybe slammed it against the couch for good measure. Then the thought occurred to me: Maybe I should get a punching bag? Minutes later, I ordered one online, and it hangs on the wall by the games in the basement to this day, a perfect place to work through all my frustration, nervousness, and overwhelm over everything from speaking at a national conference to my daughter's struggles with her homework. The kids even use it, too! It's not just about processing anger but also about releasing emotions through movement.

Being physically active is one of the best ways we can switch into the renewal phase and stay there longer. As we learned in chapters 3 and 4, uncomfortable thoughts and feelings can trigger a stress response in your brain, and your body needs your parasympathetic nervous system (which controls our ability to relax) to bring you out of fight-or-flight mode and back to a state of rest. Fortunately, many different activities can create feelings of calm, from a walk around the block to stretching your arms and legs to, yes, whaling on a punching bag. These small measures make a world of difference and protect teachers from prolonged stress that can cause serious illness over time.

WHEN IT'S HARD, IT'S AN INVITATION

I need to be honest here. It's easy to feel motivated and inspired when you're sitting here reading, but it can be a lot harder to actually live this stuff when your principal drops a last-minute faculty meeting on your plate or a parent goes off on you in a one-on-one meeting.

So what I want you to remember is this: When it gets hard, that's not a sign that you're failing at well-being. It's actually an invitation—an opportunity to put these new decisions you've made into practice.

Every challenging moment is your chance to road-test your new skills. When you feel that familiar tightness in your chest at the sight of a new email in your inbox, that's your cue to practice a breathing technique. When a colleague starts complaining and you feel yourself getting pulled into negativity, you can set a boundary and redirect the conversation, or simply leave the room.

Instead of dreading these moments, you can actually start to feel excited about them. "Bring it on, life!" becomes your rallying cry instead of "Why is this happening to me?" This shift transforms you from someone who feels victimized by the chaos of teaching into someone who feels empowered to navigate it. When you don't show up the way you want to and old habits slip back in, give yourself grace, and I promise—life will give you another invitation.

And start small. It's okay to start small! That's the only way for this to be sustainable. Pick one renewal practice and commit to it for a week. Set one boundary that feels slightly uncomfortable.

You've got this. And more important, you've got you.

MAIN TAKEAWAYS

- ✦ Like physical hygiene, your well-being requires daily attention through small, consistent actions that build up emotional reserves over time.
- ✦ You don't have control over external circumstances, but you *do* have full agency over your emotional responses. Choosing empowering feelings over disempowering ones through conscious awareness and action is huge for well-being.
- ✦ Effective boundaries aren't about controlling others: They clearly state what *you* will or won't do. Following through consistently protects your well-being, models that well-being for students and colleagues, and helps you say *yes* to what's truly aligned with your mission.
- ✦ No one gets it all right with well-being 100 percent of the time. Every time you fall off the horse, it's an invitation to give yourself grace and try again.

9

EXPAND YOUR IMPACT

In the spring of 2019, I found myself sitting in a meeting where our district was rolling out new social-emotional learning software. The administrator was walking us through all the features, explaining how teachers would monitor students' emotional well-being using digital check-ins and follow-up surveys.

As she clicked through each of the platform's various bells and whistles, explaining how we could identify struggling students and connect them with appropriate supports, I watched my colleagues' reactions.

Foreheads were furrowing . . . and eyebrows were raising. Long sighs and short huffs could be heard throughout the room. Murmurs picked up as teachers whispered their frustrations to one another: *When are we supposed to find the time for all these check-ins?*

As I took in the scene, I couldn't help but notice the irony. Here we were, a roomful of adults getting emotionally agitated about a program designed to help children . . . manage their feelings.

Finally I raised my hand. "This all sounds great for the students," I said, "but when are we rolling out the support system for the teachers?"

The question was met with laughter. The administrator looked at me like I was cracking a joke.

But I wasn't joking. When *was* the last time anyone asked how we're doing emotionally? When do *we* get check-ins and follow-up questions and appropriate supports?

The room fell silent. You could practically hear the collective realization dawning: *right*. We need that support, too.

That moment crystallized something I'd been thinking about for years. We spend a vast amount of energy trying to teach our students social-emotional skills, and yet we neglect to build and use those same skills ourselves. We're expected to be emotional first responders for hundreds of young people every day, but we've never been trained in the most essential skill of all: emotional intelligence.

In fact, we may not even know what emotional intelligence looks like in practice at all.

Imagine walking into a tense parent-teacher conference (or a meeting with your principal) and actually feeling calm and centered, knowing you can navigate whatever comes up without getting defensive, shutting down, or spiraling into a panic attack. Imagine staying regulated while a student has a full-on meltdown in your classroom and being able to respond with steadiness and grounding energy when they need it the most. Imagine hearing a snippy comment from a fellow teacher and not only *not* taking the bait but responding with empathy and trying to connect with them over what's wrong.

That is emotional intelligence in action. It's what helps us read the room when our carefully planned lesson is bombing and pivot to something that actually holds our students' attention. It's what enables us to connect and empathize with others while maintaining boundaries, to have difficult conversations without making enemies, and to model the emotional regulation we're trying to teach. It is, in short, what makes everything else that we do *work*.

The payoff extends far beyond the classroom, too. Teachers with strong emotional intelligence are going to feel energized at the end of the day instead of completely drained. They're able to leave work at work and be present with their families. They build stronger, more authentic relationships with colleagues and their students because they're not constantly on edge or taking things personally. They sleep better, worry less, and rediscover the joy that brought them to teaching in the first place. Most important, they realize they don't have to choose between being an excellent educator and having a healthy personal and emotional life.

Statements like these might feel kind of radical to us as teachers. The things that we're taught and told in our career—we're in it for the outcome, not the income; stress is just part of the job and that's that—emphasize self-sacrifice, martyrdom, setting ourselves on fire to keep others warm. So it's no wonder my question about when it would be *our* turn to look after our emotions in that roomful of teachers was met with uncomfortable laughter. But that attitude does *not* have to be something we accept without question.

What if it *doesn't* have to be all self-sacrifice? What if we *do* look after ourselves as well as our students? What if we *can* have it all?

We can. Emotional intelligence is what makes that having it all actually possible, because when you can understand and manage your own emotional landscape, you stop being at the mercy of every stressful situation and start becoming the kind of teacher—and person—you've always wanted to be.

Best of all, emotional intelligence is a trait with innate potential that we can cultivate. It's an ability that we can strengthen over time and with practice. And it's the synthesis of everything we've learned and put into practice in this book so far.

Some leadership experts consider emotional intelligence to be a soft skill (perhaps because it's nontechnical) or a "nice to have, but not essential." That is *far* from the case. There's nothing soft about managing mysterious, unpredictable, messy, complicated emotions. If anything, it's the other way around. It takes a lot of intentional, strategic work for educators to process our own feelings and then teach our students how to regulate theirs. It's not a "nice-to-have" either, but a real must, *especially* for teachers. Ultimately, no matter what subject or age group we teach, we're teaching more than just the dates of important battles in the Revolutionary War or how to solve for *x*. We're teaching students—kids—how to navigate the world as humans. How to respond when things are frustrating. How to set priorities when life feels overwhelming, and how to ask for and *extend* help. How to care for others and for ourselves. When we do that, it's because of our emotional intelligence.

In this chapter, we'll look at each of the pillars of emotional intelligence (self-awareness, self-regulation, social awareness, and relationship management), partly to learn how to better navigate the emotions that arise in ourselves and around us, and partly as a way to align all the things you've learned in this book through the lens of a well-known framework. If you're already familiar with emotional intelligence, you'll be able to make fresh connections to all the skills and concepts you've taken in over the past eight chapters and link them all together.

And if you're new to the idea of emotional intelligence (or have just kinda maybe heard of it), then you'll have a chance to learn what this buzzy (but often misunderstood) concept is all about.

UNDERSTANDING (AND AUDITING) EMOTIONAL INTELLIGENCE

Emotional intelligence (EI) is exactly what it sounds like: the ability to understand and work with emotions—both ours, and those of others. The term as we use it now was first coined by psychologists John D. Mayer and Peter Salovey in 1990,[1] but popularized by science journalist and bestselling author Daniel Goleman in his 1995 book *Emotional Intelligence: Why It Can Matter More Than IQ*,[2] and has since become a widely accepted (and studied) aspect of human behavior across the professional and personal spheres.

People with a high level of EI are compassionate and thoughtful, but still able to protect and state their own needs. They can detect someone's emotional cues and react to them without engaging their ego. They try to communicate with others instead of controlling the conversation. And most of all, they are able to connect with people on a deep level because they know how to actively listen.

The foundation of emotional intelligence rests on four pillars. The first two focus inward: self-awareness (recognizing and understanding your own emotions) and self-regulation (managing those emotions effectively). The second two look outward: social awareness (reading and understanding others' emotions) and relationship management (using that understanding to navigate interactions successfully).

If this sounds familiar, it's because those are the very skills we've been building throughout our entire journey together.

Remember when we explored metacognition and learned to notice our thought patterns? Self-awareness in action. When we practiced breathing breaks and other nervous system regulation techniques? Self-regulation. Our work on reflection and examining our biases? Social awareness. And when we learned to set boundaries and advocate effectively? Relationship management.

Now we get to put it all together under one roof.

Before we look more closely at each pillar, let's get a baseline of where you are right now. The following assessment isn't about judgment or scoring yourself; it's just a way to gather data and get a sense of how you are doing right now, in the context of today. There's always going to be room for improvement, so there's no way to fail this assessment. Remember, you can't change what you don't notice, so let's start noticing.

> You can also take this assessment online on my website at *empowerededucator.com/book*.

EMOTIONAL INTELLIGENCE SELF-ASSESSMENT

For each statement below, rate yourself on a scale from 1 to 5.

1 = Strongly Disagree

2 = Disagree

3 = Neutral

4 = Agree

5 = Strongly Agree

SELF-AWARENESS

- I can easily identify my emotions as I experience them.
- I understand how my feelings influence my behavior in the classroom.
- I am aware of the values that drive my decisions as an educator.
- I can recognize when my emotions are affecting my ability to listen to others.
- I regularly reflect on my strengths and areas for growth.

SELF-REGULATION

- I can stay calm and composed in stressful situations.
- When I notice myself getting upset, I have strategies to bring myself back to balance.
- I adapt well when unexpected changes arise.
- I can pause before reacting when a student or colleague frustrates me.
- I am intentional about maintaining healthy boundaries to protect my energy.

SOCIAL AWARENESS

- I can pick up on the emotions of others through tone, body language, or facial expression.
- I show genuine curiosity about other people's perspectives.
- I am aware of how my words and actions affect those around me.
- I can recognize when a student or colleague feels excluded or overlooked.
- I adjust my communication style based on the needs of my audience.

RELATIONSHIP MANAGEMENT

- I am skilled at building trust and rapport with colleagues and students.
- I give feedback in a way that is respectful and constructive.
- I can navigate conflict with a focus on understanding and resolution.
- I celebrate the successes of others and express appreciation often.
- I invest in relationships by listening deeply and following through on commitments.

Add up each category's score separately, then use the guide below to reflect on where you are and what to focus on next.

Score of 20–25: Strength Area

Keep nurturing it! You're already demonstrating strong skills in this area. These strengths are likely part of what makes your classroom and relationships thrive.

Here are the next steps:

- ✦ Continue practicing. Consistency matters.
- ✦ Mentor others by modeling these skills in your school community.
- ✦ Ask yourself: *How can I leverage this strength even more to create impact?*

Score of 15–19: Developing Area

This is an area to strengthen with intention. You're on your way with solid awareness and skills, but there's room for intentional growth.

Here are the next steps:

- ✦ Identify one to two specific strategies you can use in daily interactions (see the exercises throughout this chapter for ideas).
- ✦ Practice in low-stakes settings first (like with a friend or at home) to build confidence.
- ✦ Commit to a micro-shift. For example, if your social awareness score was 17, you might decide: "This week I'll pause and check in with students who seem quieter than usual."

Score 5–14: Growth Opportunity

This is an area that deserves your attention. Start small, but start now—and remember, this is not a deficit. This is simply a starting point for transformation.

Here are the next steps:

- Choose one skill in this area to focus on for the next month.
- Pair it with a daily reminder (sticky note, journal prompt, phone alarm).
- Keep track of moments where you notice even small progress so you can celebrate.
- Lean on the tools in this chapter. Pick one practice and try it consistently.
- Shift from awareness into action. For example, if you scored low in relationship management, set the goal: "I will offer one piece of genuine positive feedback each day." Small steps add up.

Finally, remember that emotional intelligence is not about achieving perfection. This is about growth over time. Treat this assessment as data, not a judgment. Every score is an opportunity to realign with your values and your vision of the teacher you want to be.

SELF-AWARENESS: WHAT'S GOING ON WITH ME RIGHT NOW?

I've said it before, and I'll say it again: We cannot change what we don't notice. Self-awareness is the cornerstone of change, because it's what gets us to the bedrock of everything that happens in our lives: *ourselves*. That's why noticing what's going on within us is the critical first pillar of emotional intelligence.

When I ask a group of teachers about how self-aware they feel, they usually fall into two camps. First, there are teachers like Kiara.

"This is mind-blowing," she said after a workshop session in which I'd outlined what self-awareness meant. "I was *going* to say that I'd describe myself as a force of nature. I am *really* good at anticipating others' needs, setting the groundwork for anyone who might need my help, and I thought that was all a product of my self-awareness. But in reality, it's like I'm aware of what everyone needs *but* me. Absolutely wild."

Teachers like Kiara are powerful advocates for their students, fiercely loyal to their colleagues, but somehow invisible to themselves. They've become so externally focused that they've forgotten they have an internal world worth paying attention to. They are falling prey to the self-sacrifice that runs so many of us ragged, pouring from the proverbial empty cup.

Then there are teachers like Natasha. "At times, I honestly feel like I'm *too* self-aware," she shared in that same workshop. "I'm micro-analyzing everything I do, second-guessing everything. It's this whole rabbit hole of *Should I have said that? Did I offend them or step on their toes? Why didn't I speak up earlier?* And it's almost paralyzing. I wish I could be *less* aware of myself sometimes."

Natasha and teachers like her are caught in a cycle of self-judgment and overthinking that *masquerades* as awareness . . . but is actually its opposite. They're so busy analyzing and critiquing their every move that they lose touch with what they're actually feeling in the moment. In other words, she is feeling self-conscious, which is inherently self-judgment. Self-awareness, on the other hand, is without judgment. Instead of noticing their emotions with curiosity and compassion, they're trapped in their heads, spinning stories about what others might think of them and falling down those rabbit holes.

What's important to understand is that—as they both realized—neither Kiara nor Natasha is practicing true self-awareness. Kiara has neglected her own inner world because she's so focused on others, while Natasha is hyperconscious of herself to the point where she freezes up.

Fortunately, both of them (and all of us) can learn to cultivate this skill. Self-awareness isn't about priding yourself on your sense of anticipating everyone's needs, nor is it obsessing over what others think of you by replaying the tape over and over in your head. It's about noticing what's happening in your body and emotions right now, in this present moment. It's about noticing when something feels aligned or misaligned, when you're moving toward your values or away from them. It's about noticing when you're powering through, overcommitting, or obsessing—with neutrality, not self-blame. It's the practice of becoming a loving, nonjudgmental observer of your own experience, without the rabbit holes or the self-abandonment.

You don't need to be mindful all the time to practice self-awareness, either. (Nobody can be 100 percent mindful of everything they do 100 percent of the time.) Remember, your body is your guide. Your body registers emotions before your conscious mind does, which is why practices like tracking your emotional state, or the Stop and Notice exercise you learned in chapter 1, are so powerful. Checking in with yourself throughout the day, asking yourself, *What is my body telling me right now?* and generally pausing to gather that data about your emotional state is all mindfulness—and self-awareness—really is.

As you develop your "notice muscle" through actions like Stop and Notice, you can work on expanding your emotional vocabulary to complement your growing self-awareness. This isn't something a lot of us are used to practicing: We're usually content to answer "Fine" when a colleague (or our partner) asks how we're doing today, and tend to generalize our reactions to events or decisions as "I feel good about this" or "*Eesh,* that went pretty badly." But being precise with how you name your emotions is foundational to emotional intelligence, and it makes a huge difference in how you *act,* too: Feeling bad because you spoke sharply to a student by mistake and feeling bad because you have a week of state testing coming up are pretty different scenarios, and understanding the nuances is where the real self-awareness kicks in.

In short, the more precisely you can name your emotions, the better equipped you'll be to respond to them constructively.

Exercise: The Feelings Wheel

When you notice a feeling arising, try using the feelings wheel below to get more specific about what you're actually experiencing. Are you angry or are you frustrated? Disappointed? Resentful?

This isn't just a glorified thesaurus, either; the difference matters, because each emotion gives you different information about what you need. For instance, *frustration* might signal that you need to adjust your approach to a problem to make real headway on it, while *resentment* might indicate that a boundary has been crossed and you need to reaffirm it with the other person. You can find a printable PDF of the Feelings Wheel at *empowerededucator.com/book*.

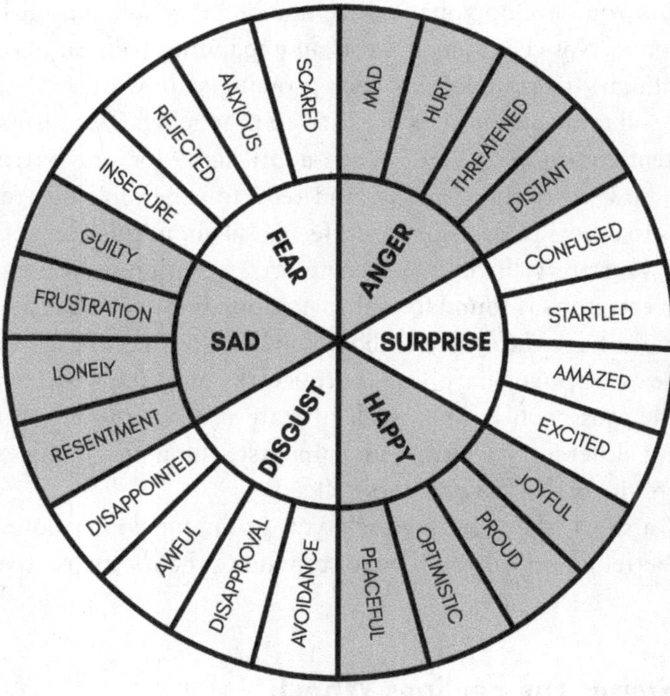

FIGURE 4: FEELINGS WHEEL

SELF-REGULATION: WHAT DO I NEED TO DO FOR MYSELF?

We've talked about self-regulation a *lot* in this book (because it's pretty important), but here's where it all comes together. As a pillar of emotional intelligence, self-regulation isn't just about managing your stress in the moment, surviving the chaos of your classroom, or making it through another faculty meeting. It's about consciously choosing how you want to show up in every interaction, every day, and understanding what you need to do in order to be who you want to be. It's not enough to just take a deep breath and hope for the best (though breathing breaks are definitely part of it). Effective self-regulation requires you to first *identify the emotional pattern*, then *regulate the emotion*, and finally *reframe the situation*. Trying to skip straight to reframing—thinking your way out of feeling bad—is emotional bypassing, and it doesn't work.

Liza is an elementary school teacher and a self-admitted "reformed emotional bypasser." Liza's issue was internalizing her class's daily behavior as a measure of how they felt about her . . . and usually feeling pretty crummy about it. "I love kids—like, it's the whole reason I do this job!" she told me. "So to think that they didn't like me really hurt my heart."

For a while, Liza's way of dealing with this was to jump right to a kind of reframe: *Well, fine,* she'd tell herself, *I'm not here to be liked. I'm here to teach.* But that didn't really help her get in touch with the emotional pattern she was operating under, let alone help her regulate how she was feeling when those emotions got stirred up. It definitely didn't make her feel any better, either.

And the kicker? Liza wasn't even right. Some of her students actually came back to visit long after graduation, and all of them made a point to tell her how much they loved her class. Turns out that their acting up had *nothing* to do with her.

Now Liza does things differently. Instead of jumping straight to *I'm not here to be liked, so who cares anyway?* she's learned to pause and acknowledge what's actually happening in her body: her chest getting tight, her pulse picking up. Then she uses the self-regulation tools we've been practicing throughout this book to get herself feeling calm and grounded again.

From there, Liza has been able to identify her emotional patterns around these incidents. In her reactive state, she was someone who took everything personally, who made her students' behavior about her own worth. But who she *wanted* to be was something different: a teacher who felt grounded and empowered even when things were chaotic around her. (Which ultimately led her to create and follow through with more effective classroom management strategies!)

Our minds (and particularly our egos) love to make meaning out of everything. However, this meaning can sometimes lead to downward spirals of worry and anxiety. Everything objectively *is*, simply and entirely, *until* your mind creates meaning. When that happens, your interpretation of an event becomes your experience.

In other words, everything is inherently neutral. To paraphrase something I learned from professional coach and neurosomatics expert Tracy Litt: *Your heart beats, the sun shines, the wind blows, and* [fill in the blank]. For example:

> *My heart beats, the sun shines, the wind blows, and my students misbehaved today.*
>
> *My heart beats, the sun shines, the wind blows, and I totally flopped on my observation.*
>
> *My heart beats, the sun shines, the wind blows, and my colleagues are not collaborating with me.*

See how these statements just *are*? Cultivating this kind of neutrality about the reality of things is a powerful way to help yourself reframe the situation or at the very least get out of the disempowering feedback loop. That's what Liza did when teasing apart the neutral reality of her situation (her students were misbehaving) from the meaning she drew from it.

SOCIAL AWARENESS: WHAT ARE THE PEOPLE AROUND ME FEELING?

One of my favorite books about social awareness is *If I Understood You, Would I Have This Look on My Face?* written by Alan Alda (the guy from *M*A*S*H*).[3] As the title suggests, the book is brilliant, fun, *and* very thoughtful about how we're presenting ourselves and how we pick up on what other people are thinking and feeling through signs and signals.

In the book, Alda talks about a kind of game he plays with himself when he's out and about—like at the grocery store, waiting in line to check out. He'll observe the people around him—their expressions, their posture—and try to get a sense of what they might be feeling, what emotions are running through them in the moment.

This is a great example of what social awareness can look like. When you're people watching, tuning into the feelings on display in a TV show or in a movie, or picking up on the vibes in a room, you're exercising your ability to understand the emotional signals of others around you. Understanding emotions in others helps us build empathy, navigate relationships, and respond appropriately to the people around us—in other words, use our emotional intelligence

The simplest way to build your social awareness muscle is just like Alan Alda did: by observing strangers and trying to tune into what they're feeling based on clues like body language, facial expressions, tone of voice, and the language that people use.

You can also practice by becoming more aware of the energy of groups of people—by essentially reading the room. We've all walked into a space and immediately felt the emotional tone shift. Maybe you can tell when someone walks into a room if they're sucking all the oxygen out of the space or if they're carrying a lot of magnetic energy. That's because your energy speaks before you even open your mouth. Reading the room when you walk into a space is about being curious: *Hmm, what is the emotional tone of this room right now? What's the vibe here?* Again, the answers to these questions are never black-and-white; it's the act of noticing itself that kicks your social awareness into gear.

Exercise: Observation Without Judgment

During your next faculty meeting, try this simple observation exercise. Look around the room and start to notice people's:

Body language—posture, gestures, energy level

Facial expressions—micro-expressions, eye contact

Tone of voice—warmth, tension, enthusiasm, hesitation

Group dynamics—who talks more, who stays quiet, who is leaning in or pulling back

There's also more to social awareness than sitting back and passively observing others' emotions. To be clear, we can never be 100 percent sure of what someone else is thinking and feeling, after all (like when someone has—ahem—resting witch face). And of course our own perceptions of things like facial expressions are filtered through our personal biases. Social awareness also involves how we listen to others in conversations and relationships, which can be surprisingly difficult. We often assume we're good at listening (kind of like how everyone thinks they're a good driver!) and think of *listening* as a simple soft skill that we just . . . know how to do. But at the same time, it's so easy to be sitting there, nodding attentively, eyes focused, but really just tuned into your own internal monologue.

Fortunately, it's a habit we *can* break if we come at it with intention. So in the name of social awareness, let's all commit to listening for understanding more than just listening until it's our turn to speak.

Finally, social awareness in its broadest sense means looking for the whole picture. It means realizing—and *accepting*—that everyone's truth is true for them. It's like that diagram where there's two people looking at a number from opposite sides: one person sees a six, so the person on the other side sees a nine. Who's right? Who's *wrong*? Well . . . both and neither, right? It's all a matter of perspective. And as my friend John always asks, is it more important to be *right* or to build a relationship with the other person based on authentic curiosity? Social awareness is the ability to recognize that people experience and interpret situations differently based on their vantage points and to respond to them with empathy and attunement.

RELATIONSHIP MANAGEMENT: WHAT DO I NEED TO DO TO CONNECT WITH OTHERS?

Now we arrive at the fourth and final pillar of emotional intelligence: relationship management.

As educators, we don't work in isolation. Teaching is an inherently social line of work—it's at *least* you and one other person. More often than not, we're interacting with dozens of people every day and forging relationships with all of them: students who test our patience, colleagues who see things differently than we do, administrators who make decisions we don't understand, and parents who sometimes make our jobs complicated. (And that's just at work. At home, we have our own families, friends, and communities that require our attention and care.)

Every single one of these relationships has the potential to either energize us or drain us completely (and to do the same for the other person, too). The difference often comes down to how we show up in those interactions—in other words, how we manage those relationships. When we're skillful in our relationship management, we can respond thoughtfully to others' emotions. We can leave interactions feeling energized and empowered, or neutral, or—if we do notice we're activated—feeling equipped for what to do next. We're self-assured (but not pushy) and curious (but not nosy or judgmental). We can set and maintain boundaries without building walls or getting defensive, and we can know how to circle back when we don't show up as our best selves (which is inevitable—we're only human, after all).

All of this starts by recognizing a truth we've hit on several times: To manage relationships well, we have to give up judgment and check our ego at the door.

Now, even though this is well-covered territory by now, I'm not going to pretend this is simple. It's *very* easy to say *avoid judgment* and much harder to do it. So here's a bit of emotional intelligence truth to help you out: *All judgment is self-judgment.* When you get curious about your judgmental thoughts, it turns out that they very often reveal something about your *own* fears, insecurities, or unmet needs. Maybe you're judging that parent as demanding because you're worried about your own ability to meet expectations. Maybe you're frustrated with your dramatic colleague because you're feeling overwhelmed and wish you felt as comfortable speaking up as she does. In making these judgments, your ego is jumping into the fray in an attempt to stabilize the status quo and justify why *they're* wrong and *you're* right. (Remember, your ego is actually trying to keep you safe by maintaining your sense of who you are—no matter what.)

Once you start to see judgment as information about *yourself* rather than facts about other people, everything changes. You open yourself to self-reflection (as we discussed in chapter 5) rather than jumping to conclusions—because judgment and curiosity can't exist in the same space. So when you notice those judgmental thoughts creeping in (and they will), start asking questions. When a colleague launches into a vocal complaint about some new policy, try replacing your thought of *Ugh, she's being dramatic again,* with *Isn't that interesting? I wonder why this is so important to her.* When your principal brushes off your concern for the umpteenth time, instead of *He never listens to anyone,* try *I'm noticing that I'm feeling frustrated. What's going on here?*

Once we can let go of judgment more easily, we're that much more open to communication—obviously, a very important part of relationship management. As is true with listening, most of us think we're way better at communicating than we actually are. Just as we think that we're listening because we can hear the words coming out of someone's mouth, we assume that responding with our own take on the situation counts as communicating. But real communication—the kind that builds relationships and solves problems, the kind that's powered by emotional intelligence—is a more nuanced skill. It requires us to do more than simply take a person's words at face value and invites us to be curious about the why behind their statements, opinions, and arguments.

When I do live workshops, I like to illustrate this deeper

kind of communication with a little partner exercise. I'll pair everyone off, give them a topic to discuss, and ask one person to explain why they *love* this thing and the other one to explain why they *don't* love this thing (even if they're just pretending for the sake of the exercise). For example, I might give them the topic of shopping malls, and the exchange then goes something like this:

> **Person A: I love shopping malls because I like to get all my things in one place.**
>
> **Person B: Well, I hate shopping malls because I don't like having to drive out somewhere and try to find parking.**
>
> **Person A: Okay, well, I love shopping malls because they're a good place to do something fun with my friends.**
>
> **Person B: Well, I *hate* shopping malls because I don't like all the people around me.**

This back-and-forth is just opinion tennis, each person stating their view without really listening or understanding the other. Once they've batted the conversational ball over the net a few times, I move to the second part of the exercise.

This time around, I ask each person to check for understanding after their partner states their opinion. This can be as simple as saying "So what you're saying is . . ." and filling in the blank with a synthesis of what they said. At this point, the conversation is more like this:

> **Person A: I love shopping malls because I can get all my stuff in one place.**

Person B: So what you're saying is you value convenience when you go shopping.

Person A: Yeah, it *is* convenient. And I think I like getting out of the house and socializing, too.

Person B: See, I hate shopping malls because there are so many crowds.

Person A: So what you're saying is you prefer to shop somewhere less crowded because a lot of people overwhelm you.

Person B: No, it's not that I feel overwhelmed, actually—I just really dislike all the germs.

See how much more understanding—from both sides—comes through with just that small tweak? (And how in that second example, the understanding was actually *inaccurate* initially until Person A checked with Person B?) Actively listening in this way is a huge game changer, and it's something that comes more and more naturally as you build up your emotional intelligence. And what's most fascinating is what goes on *visually* during this exercise: People's shoulders drop. Their facial expressions relax. Their posture generally becomes more open and engaged.

Why? Because most of us walk around feeling like nobody really gets us. When someone takes the time to not just hear our words, but understand our meaning, it feels like a gift. So practice giving that gift to others—you might be surprised how easily you get it back.

Exercise: Listening for Understanding

Try this the next time you're in a conversation with someone who's sharing something important. Instead of immediately jumping to your response or your advice or your similar experience, pause and say, "So what I'm hearing is . . ." and then reflect back not just their words, but the feeling or value or concern underneath them.

That said, make sure you're not just repeating exactly what they say, verbatim (or even paraphrased). You want to synthesize and ask questions, not just echo back. If you follow the words "So what you're saying is . . ." with a transcript of what they just said, you're playing a tape recorder, not listening. (I had a professor in grad school who did this, and it drove me up a wall . . . even though I know she was *trying* to listen actively.) When you synthesize, you're proving you understood the person *and* you're trying to gain further understanding by making educated guesses about their whys.

Relationship management isn't *just* about having these engaged, connective conversations, however. If you're human and you work with other humans, you're going to have conflict from time to time. The question isn't whether it will happen; it's whether it will be destructive or productive, and emotional intelligence is what will make the difference.

The first part of emotionally intelligent conflict management is simply accepting that conflict does happen *and* that it doesn't have to be zero-sum. (Two things can be true at the same time!) Remember that example with the two people standing at opposite ends of the number—one saw a 6, one saw a 9? Our different perspectives are bound to cause friction sometimes. Framing conflict as something inherently bad or as the result of "doing things wrong" is counterproductive and often comes from how we learned about conflict when we grew up. The good news is, since these are learned reactions and responses, we can *unlearn* them when they're not working and learn new, empowered skills to navigate with.

Similarly, emotional intelligence means letting go of the notion that conflict is a *contest*. So many of us take it for granted that conflict means someone is going to win and someone is going to lose. It's you in one corner and the other person—your opponent—in the other, ready to duke it out like Rocky and Apollo Creed.

But let me just ask you: How's that approach working out? Because it certainly leaves *me* feeling drained and anxious, and it sure doesn't improve any of my relationships.

The emotionally intelligent approach to conflict is not to deny it or lock in for a knock-down, drag-out fight. It's to *reframe* the conflict as "us versus the problem" instead of "me versus you." Instead of griping that your principal always schedules meetings during your planning period (or tearing into them for not respecting your time), you can say, "I'm hoping we can solve a problem together. I'm struggling to balance the meeting schedule with my class preparation time. Can we figure out a way to make both things work?" Instead of calling out a student for being disruptive and trying to will them into buckling down, try saying, "Hey, looks like it's hard to focus today! How can we make it easier for you?"

When you frame conflicts this way, you're looking for common ground instead of battle lines—and most of the time, you can find it. Even if you can't quite get there, you can fall back on the rest of your emotional intelligence (self-awareness, self-regulation, and social awareness) to help keep things grounded and moving forward rather than spinning out.

DIFFICULT CONVERSATIONS

Here's another thing nobody teaches you about difficult conversations: It's okay to admit that they're difficult. In fact, it's helpful. If you're nervous about a conversation you need to have, it's okay to say so. "I need to talk to you about something, and I'm feeling a little nervous about it. I'm hoping we can both come out of this feeling heard." If you're feeling emotional about a situation, acknowledge it. "This situation has been really frustrating for me, and I want to make sure I can explain that clearly without getting too worked up." When you start a difficult conversation with transparency about your own state of mind, you do two important things. First, you model vulnerability, which often makes the other person feel safer to be vulnerable, too, creating another bridge for connection. Second, you give them context for understanding your perspective and an invitation to come to the conversation more open-minded.

ASSUMPTIONS OF UNCONDITIONAL POSITIVE REGARD

Here's an invitation for you, even if it feels ridiculous at first: Assume that everyone is doing the best they can.

I know, I know. You're probably thinking about that colleague who always seems to have a catty comment at the ready, or that student who insists on "hiding" their earbuds under their hoodie even though you've told them not to a thousand times and wants to engage in a power struggle, or even the driver on your commute who cuts you off at a yellow light. *I'm supposed to think that* they're *doing their best?*

Well, I can't *prove* to you that everyone is always doing their best. But it is a choice I consciously make about how I want to see the world, and that choice makes my life significantly better. So yes, this is an opportunity for you to experience something more expansive that invites in possibility, potential, and connection.

This is unconditional positive regard, and it's what I believe is at the heart of relationship management.

Unconditional positive regard means we choose (because it's an active decision on our part) to see everyone, no matter what, as doing the best they can with what they have. It's not a pure Pollyanna, sprinkling glitter over everything, turn-that-frown-upside-down emotional bypass. It's simply acknowledging that nobody wakes up in the morning thinking, *I can't* wait *to be a huge pain in everyone's ass today.* It's also not an excuse for bad behavior (that is, it's not saying that harmful actions won't have consequences); it's going through your day knowing that people are generally doing the best they can with the resources, information, and emotional capacity they have in that moment. It's knowing that all people, everywhere, are just *people.*

In that sense, it's a profound way to see the world. It's a kind of exercise in affirming human dignity, remembering that no matter what we do or how we do it, we're ultimately all trying to get through the day, keep ourselves safe, and express who we are.

When you start from that assumption, you approach every interaction with more curiosity and less defensiveness. You operate with greater and broader emotional intelligence. And you can actually start to shift things around you.

Because the beautiful thing about emotional intelligence isn't just how it makes your life easier and makes you feel more empowered in the moment. It's how it creates positive ripple effects everywhere you go. When you are tuned into your own feelings, when you show up with curiosity instead of judgment, when you listen in order to understand instead of just waiting for your turn to talk, when you assume good intentions instead of the worst, you change the energy of every room you enter.

Your students feel safer to take risks and make mistakes. Your colleagues feel more comfortable collaborating with you, confiding in you, and being their authentic selves around you. Your administrators are more likely to trust your insights. Your family feels more connected to you.

Unconditional positive regard is a mindset, but it leads us to real actions—and a powerful path for connection. When you see people through the lens of unconditional positive regard, you start to tune in more and more to the ways in which they make the world better, to how *they* are doing their best out there, and when you reflect what *they're* doing back to them, it makes both of you feel more connected. These moments of reflection and appreciation can be small, but their impact isn't.

That's what I invite you to do now: Take some time to reflect your appreciation or admiration to someone you see doing their best. Send a text to a colleague telling them you're grateful for something they did. Write a note to a student who's been struggling. Call a friend just to check in. Practice gratitude by telling someone specifically what they bring to your life.

These might seem like tiny things, but they're profound acts of relationship building. Every time you choose connection over isolation, understanding over judgment, curiosity over defensiveness, you're not just improving that one interaction, but becoming the kind of person who makes every space a little bit better.

MAIN TAKEAWAYS

- Emotional intelligence is the ability to understand and work with emotions—our own and those of others. It draws on all the skills and concepts you've learned so far in this book and rests on four pillars: self-awareness, self-regulation, social awareness, and relationship management.
- Self-awareness is the skill of being able to notice what we're feeling and put words to it. It's a nonjudgmental practice of neutral curiosity that invites us to take a look at what we're feeling (and how that shows up in our body) without self-criticism or blame.
- Self-regulation is consciously choosing how you want to show up in your interactions in order to be who you want to be. It invites you to identify the emotional pattern, regulate the emotion, and (optionally) reframe the situation.
- Social awareness is about tuning into the feelings of others—without judgment or presumption. Understanding the emotional signals of those around you is the bedrock of building empathy and responding appropriately to other people.

- Relationship management rests on perspective-taking and curiosity. When we can release judgment of others (because all judgment is secretly *self*-judgment), we can take ourselves out of the equation, listen for understanding, and practice unconditional positive regard—all of which paves the way for real connection.

10

CELEBRATE YOUR AGENCY

Think of a typical Sunday during the school year. You wake up, maybe after you have slept in (a little) or have hit the ground running with chores and family duties. By midday, you're probably tackling some things on your to-do list, knocking out the grocery shopping for the week or catching up on house repairs, lawn care, and those projects you keep avoiding. But as the day turns into afternoon and then into early evening, the familiar feeling starts to creep in. Maybe you're sitting on your couch, scrolling through your phone and half watching TV. Maybe your phone buzzes with a reminder or email notification. Maybe you simply glimpse the clock that reads 4:30 p.m. and your chest tightens a little. *Seriously? Where did the weekend go?* Your mind begins its weekly inventory of everything you need to remember for Monday—the tests you haven't graded, the laundry you haven't done, the lesson plans that exist only as bullet points in your head—and your heart starts to ache with the sense of freedom slipping away. The weekends never seem long enough to get everything done, and the genuine rest you crave feels like a pipe dream.

But what if Sunday could feel *entirely different?*

What if your Sunday could be completely restorative? What if Sundays could actually be a *celebration*?

Instead of beginning your week feeling as if you're already behind the ball, your end-of-weekend evenings are the perfect time to do this last vital part of feeling truly empowered: the Sunday SHIFT.

This simple acronym—*sense*, *honor*, *integrate*, *focus*, and *transform*—is a short, easy set of thought exercises you can make part of your routine at the end of your weekend to reinvite yourself to be curious, reframe, and—yes—celebrate. It's a handy way to incorporate everything you now know, and it can be the perfect antidote to those creeping feelings of anxiety and overwhelm that tend to creep up on us before we plunge into a new school week (aka the Sunday Scaries).

Because how great would it be to start your week feeling amazing? How great would it feel to start your week celebrating yourself?

That's what the Sunday SHIFT can do.

Celebration is an essential piece of the puzzle of our work here—not simply the icing on the cake, but more like the heat of the oven that transforms the raw ingredients into something more than the sum of their parts. Celebration cements our sense of success—because we *are* achieving success when we do this work. It inspires us to do more, sustainably and thoughtfully. And, when we carry the energy it gives us into our week, it can bring together our community of educators to empower *one another*. As teachers, we *need* to celebrate our wins, both massive and tiny, because celebration is what creates the will to keep going, collectively *and* individually.

But self-celebration can feel uncomfortable. As a culture,

we have a tendency to deflect celebration when it's directed at ourselves. We might have been told that it's rude to toot your own horn. You don't want to be too loud, too bold, or too shiny because it might make other people feel bad. Ideas like tall poppy syndrome—that anyone who sticks out (i.e., is a tall poppy) gets cut down—may have taught us that sticking out for any reason, even if it was for our accomplishments and our genuine wins, was a problem, and might have earned us a scolding, a cold shoulder from our friends, or at least some side-eyes.

We often have a knee-jerk reaction to minimize any recognition we do get. Someone compliments your new blazer? "Oh, it was on sale." A parent says they like your bulletin board display? "I just copied it from Pinterest." It can feel impossible to even receive a compliment or praise without some sort of response that reduces the sentiment. It seems as if we treat joy and celebration as if we are undeserving. But of course you *are* deserving.

And since you've reached this section in the book, you can see what's possible when you are no longer available to stay small and feel unworthy. The truth is, your celebration of self can have an impact on everyone around you—including your colleagues and your students. Celebration and joy are like the flame on a candlewick. If you use one bright candle to light another candle, the first candle doesn't go out; it burns just as brightly—and the second one does, too. So let's SHINE.

That said, while of course it feels good to celebrate, celebration isn't just patting ourselves on the back for a quick mood boost. It's actually a culmination of all the skills and strategies you've put together in this book.

Think back to your vision from chapter 2—that detailed picture of how you want to feel and who you want to be.

Celebration is how you acknowledge progress toward that vision, how you mark the moments when you're living it, even imperfectly. Without celebration, your vision remains abstract, something you'll achieve "someday." With celebration, it becomes alive in your daily experience when you recognize and affirm the ways in which you're living it already. Did you have the hard conversation? Celebrate! Did you spend twenty minutes doing something you care about instead of unconsciously scrolling on your phone? Celebrate! Did you decide to sleep in on Sunday because you made rest a priority? Celebrate!

Remember the nervous system regulation work from chapter 1 (and the in-depth details from chapter 9)? Celebration creates the neurochemical conditions that support regulation. In doing so, your brain releases dopamine and serotonin, and if you're sharing it with other people, oxytocin. This cocktail doesn't just make you feel good; it makes your brain want to repeat the behaviors that led to the celebration. It's how you wire yourself for more of what you actually want and continue to recommit to the work.

Here's what I've learned after working with thousands of educators (and practicing this work myself): Every other practice in this book—boundary setting, nervous system regulation, reflection, emotional intelligence—will eventually fade without recommitment via celebration. You'll read about breathwork and never do it. You'll understand your triggers and still react to them. You'll start to set boundaries and let them crumble. Not because you don't want to or are uninterested, but because sustainable change requires continuous recommitment with positive reinforcement. It requires celebration. It requires *joy.*

So let's celebrate together. Let's turn the Sunday Scaries at the end of your week into a time you look forward to eagerly and with excitement.

Let's SHIFT.

SENSE—HOW AM I FEELING RIGHT NOW?

Start by finding a quiet spot where you can sit by yourself for a few moments. This first step is about the intention (internal) of your attention (external). There are so many things calling out for your attention, but you need to think of your attention as currency. You have a limited amount of attentive resources. So if you're being honest with yourself, where are you placing your attention? Sensing is how you reconnect with your body and practice moving your attention to where you want it to be. Remember, you can't change what you don't notice, so if you don't feel as if you have agency over your attention, nothing will ever change. This is another way to put Complete Personal Responsibility (CPR) into practice.

Place your phone in another room; this is your time to check in with your body. The first step to SHIFT starts with the Stop and Notice exercise and a box breath (use either version in chapter 1 or listen to one of the resources at *empowerededucator.com/book*). Notice where you're holding any tension. Are your shoulders or jaw tight or relaxed? Is your chest open or are your shoulders hunched? Is your breathing steady and deep or shallow? Remember, it's not about fixing anything. Your body is constantly giving you information; this is just your chance to listen. Sense what you're feeling.

Then as you turn your thoughts to the week ahead, notice what comes up emotionally and physically and get curious. If you feel a flutter in your stomach thinking about the next few days, lean in and ask yourself what's up. Maybe you're genuinely looking forward to introducing your next lesson or to watching your students' presentations, and your body is reflecting that excitement physically. Or maybe you're feeling some anxiety around that admin observation on Tuesday or that IEP meeting on Friday, and your body's sending you a different signal. There are no wrong answers, even if the feelings you're noticing seem to be disempowering ones at first.

HONOR—SELF-COMPASSION WITHOUT JUDGMENT

Now that you've sensed how you're feeling, the next step is to honor those feelings without immediately rushing to fix, change, or improve them. This is where many of us get stuck. We become aware of our anxiety about the upcoming week and instantly start strategizing about how to eliminate it, or we notice we're feeling depleted and immediately pile on guilt about not being "stronger."

What if, instead, you remembered that feelings are data? What if you treated them as information to *honor*?

Perhaps that Sunday-evening anxiety isn't a character flaw but a signal that there's something that needs your attention. What if feeling tired after a full week isn't evidence that you're weak, but a sign that you need to rest or prioritize your restoration?

This is where you can move from a place of self-pity to self-compassion and grace. Notice your language and go back to chapter 7. Your internal monologue is very powerful. Self-compassion sounds like: "This is really challenging right now, and it makes sense that I'm feeling anxious [or fill in the blank with whatever you're feeling]. What do I need to support myself through this?" It acknowledges the difficulty while maintaining your agency and resilience.

Self-compassion doesn't mean lowering your standards or making excuses, either. As you've learned, it means treating yourself with the same kindness you'd show a beloved friend facing the same situation—to let your Inner Bestie take the mic instead of your Inner Bully.

As you reflect on the past week, practice honoring both your struggles and your growth without passing judgment on how you did. This isn't about keeping score or proving you're good enough. It's about developing the ability to hold the full spectrum of your experience with compassion. You can celebrate the lesson that went beautifully and the tough conversation that ended up productive and respectful, while acknowledging the last-period class that felt like a disaster—often these are all part of the same week (or even the same day).

Your feelings about the upcoming week also deserve validation, even the uncomfortable ones. If you're feeling uneasy about parent-teacher conferences, for example, that uneasiness isn't irrational—it's information. Perhaps it's your relationship management skills at work. Perhaps it's a signal you're taking something personally that you can let go of. If you're dreading the staff meeting, perhaps that dread is pointing to something important about what you need in your work environment and a boundary you need to set. All emotions carry wisdom when we honor them instead of dismissing them.

YOU CAN'T MESS THIS UP

It's important to remember that while all the steps of this practice can help you move out of a default Sunday Scaries mode every week, emotions do not need to be fixed. Some feelings just need time and space to be felt. So if you try the SHIFT framework and still feel that end-of-the-weekend melancholy sometimes, it's okay.

> You haven't done it wrong. Give yourself the grace that you so easily extend to others. Every week (or every day) is a new invitation to try it again and see what comes up.

So as you move through this part of your Sunday SHIFT, ask yourself: What do I need to honor about this past week? Maybe you need to honor how hard you tried when that lesson didn't go as planned. Maybe you need to honor the courage it took to have that difficult conversation with a colleague. Maybe you need to honor the growth you've experienced, even if it came through struggle.

And what do you need to honor about your feelings toward the upcoming week? Maybe you need to honor your excitement about the new unit you're starting. Maybe you need to honor your apprehension about a challenging situation you'll need to navigate. All of it deserves acknowledgment. All of it is part of your very human experience of caring deeply about work that matters.

INTEGRATE—REGULATE YOUR NERVOUS SYSTEM

As you know, your emotional awareness and physical regulation are two sides of the same coin. When you noticed that tension in your shoulders or that flutter of excitement in your chest, your body was giving you information about your emotional state. Now you get to use that information to create the kind of calm, grounded feeling in your body that makes everything else possible by thoughtfully regulating your nervous system.

Remember, self-regulation isn't one-size-fits-all—how you need to regulate on a Sunday evening when you're feeling depleted from a week of testing might be different from the in-the-moment exercises you practice when you feel triggered at work.

Are you feeling that familiar Sunday worry that makes your jaw tight and your thoughts race? Try some intentional breathing—make your exhale longer than your inhale to signal to your parasympathetic nervous system that you're safe. Feel your shoulders drop and your whole system settle into calm alertness.

If you're feeling scattered or overwhelmed by everything you need to remember for the week, this might be the perfect moment to put your hand on your heart and simply notice your breath.

If you're really feeling those Sunday Scaries, engage your sense of hope (remember the renewal exercises from chapter 8?). Use your imagination to connect with something positive you're moving toward: maybe a favorite book you'll be reading with your class, or even just the satisfaction you'll feel when you've navigated the week with intention.

If you're carrying physical tension from the week or feeling that restless Sunday energy, movement might be exactly what you need. This could be as simple as stretching your arms overhead, taking a walk around the block, or even doing some jumping jacks in your bedroom. Movement helps shift you out of mental loops and into your body, where regulation happens.

No matter how you decide to regulate, the key is choosing what serves you in this moment, not what you think you should do. That's how you bring yourself back *to* yourself.

FOCUS—INTENTIONAL DIRECTION FOR THE WEEK

We teachers love a good list, and making a little pre-week plan might already be part of your routine. This, though, is slightly different. This isn't about the tasks, meetings, and lessons you have to tackle, but about how you want to show up for all of it and where you choose to put your energy. This part of your Sunday SHIFT has two parts: identifying the feeling you want to have and choosing a priority.

Part 1: Ask yourself how you want to feel over the next five days. Think about picking out your feelings the same way you think about what clothes to wear. What feelings do you want to try on this week?

If you decide that you want to feel connected, maybe you go into Wednesday's faculty meeting with the intention of talking with the colleagues you don't usually see during the day instead of going on autopilot, leaving you feeling drained and desperate for some alone time. Maybe you want to jump into the first day of Science Club with energy and enthusiasm instead of stress and frazzledness. Maybe you simply want to end the week feeling calm and grounded instead of fried and cranky. Choose two to three emotions that will be your North Star for the week.

Part 2: With that focus in mind, you can start to plan your priority (and yes, that's priority, singular). From your place of regulation and clarity about how you want to feel, choose one main priority for the week and the actions you can take to achieve it. Here's where we look at a priority less in terms of *What's the most urgent thing for external deadlines?* and more in terms of *What's the most important thing I want to do considering how I want to feel for myself and the vision I'm creat-*

ing? This is how you start to move the needle toward your vision with intention.

If you want to feel joy, maybe that means your priority is to honor your commitment not to gossip and complain during lunch. If you want to feel energized, not stressed, about that day of Science Club, maybe you block out some time for a grounding exercise or two before you walk into the classroom. If you want to feel calm instead of cranky, maybe it's prioritizing a short gratitude exercise every day.

This isn't about trying to make yet another to-do list or demanding that you lock in on your goals. It's about being intentional with how you take actions to direct your emotional energy. If you move through your week seeing everything as a priority, nothing is a priority. When you choose your feelings and one meaningful priority, you transform from someone who's just gritting their teeth and hanging on until Friday into someone who's designing their daily experience and navigating their week with real intention.

TRANSFORM—CELEBRATE AND RECOMMIT

Finally, it's party time!

Let's break out the streamers and balloons, because this is where we've been heading all along. One of my favorite things I do with the educators I work with is something my team and I call Yay Me's. Recently, I used this exercise with a roomful of school administrators in California. After introductions, I told them we were going to celebrate ourselves—something big or little. Anything from "I only pressed the snooze button twice" to "I ran a 5K." When I said, "Go!" the whole group filled with smiles, laughter, and cheers: *I finally booked that dentist appointment—yay me! I put my dog's food on auto-ship—yay me! My divorce is finalized—YAY ME!* (That last one got a huge round of applause.)

For the last part of your Sunday SHIFT, write out five Yay Me's for the week. If it feels aligned, you can also create some kind of celebration ritual for yourself: a victory anthem you blast for a mini dance party (my kids know that Pink is always playing on Sundays!), or writing your win on a sticky note and adding it to a "Yes, I did that!" jar. These celebratory experiences can help your brain latch on to the feeling of recognition more easily the more you practice it.

Although they seem light (and maybe a bit fluffy at first), Yay Me's are powerful. And while this is an important last step to your Sunday SHIFT, you can also extend your Yay Me practice into each day. Pick a routine action you do almost every day—hitting your car's ignition, turning the lights of your classroom on and off—and use that as your reminder to give yourself a quick Yay Me. *I had a tough conversation with a parent today—yay me. I took a nap when I needed it—yay me. I finished my grading before nine p.m.—yay me.* Or try it in small groups at a faculty meeting—or even with your students. What would change in your school environment if people felt comfortable celebrating themselves?

The beauty of this practice is that it creates momentum that builds on itself. Each week your celebrations become fuel for more growth, and your recommitments become invitations for more joy. Before you know it, Sunday evenings stop feeling like the end of freedom and start feeling like the beginning of possibility—a weekly reminder that you get to choose, again and again, how you want to show up in the world.

Exercise: Sunday SHIFT Weekly Prompts

Here's a quick and simple rundown of the prompts you can use for your own Sunday SHIFT. Give yourself the gift of ten to twenty minutes each Sunday in a quiet space to do this exercise. Write it in your calendar so you remember. Make this commitment to yourself.

Sense: Find a quiet place and start with a body scan. How am I feeling right now? How do I feel about the upcoming week?

Honor: Lean in and feel without judgment. What do I need to honor about this past week and the week to come? What needs attention?

Integrate: What do I need to do right now to feel regulated and grounded?

Focus: What is my intention for the week? How do I want to feel? What is my priority?

Transform: What can I celebrate about this past week? Which practices am I recommitting to?

For a quick-start guide to all the prompts in the Sunday SHIFT and other ways to incorporate the SHIFT process, visit the resources at *empowerededucator.com/book*.

THE LEGACY OF YOUR SHIFT

One evening after dinner, my daughter, Sandra, and I went for a walk as we usually do. She was going into the sixth grade at the time and was talking about which of her classmates were going to have a glow-up after summer. She had just turned eleven and loved her new status as a tween. As we walked and talked, she paused for a moment and looked at me.

"Mom," she said. "You know what? A glow-up isn't really about what you look like on the outside. It's about your confidence and how you feel on the inside. When you feel good about yourself, other people feel it, too." I wish I'd had that type of clarity when I was her age.

Here's the thing: I'm not sitting my kids down for regular pop quizzes on emotional intelligence or self-regulation. I don't give them worksheets on boundary setting or flash cards on the different parts of the nervous system. Unless it comes up in conversation, we're not necessarily talking about it directly.

They've learned by watching. They learned because I modeled for them. They learned because we are always teaching (especially when we think they're not looking). And when we're empowered within and for ourselves, we have so, so much to offer.

Since starting this work, I've seen my kids show up in their own friendships with the ability to graciously but firmly set boundaries (so critical in those years of intense playground drama). I've seen them pause and take deep breaths when they need it. I've watched them use their voice and advocate for themselves. I've seen them think about who they want to be in this world and how they want to feel while navigating it. I've seen them make mistakes and I've witnessed them making things right. I've celebrated their Yay Me's with them.

That, to me, is what this is all about.

This work isn't simply about solving stress and overwhelm. It's something bigger, something we need to celebrate here at the end of this book: the ripple effect that extends far beyond your classroom walls. Your legacy as an empowered educator.

Because the same way you are always teaching, your students are always learning.

They're observing how you handle stress, how you respond to conflict, how you treat yourself when you make mistakes. When you show up as an emotionally regulated, empowered adult, you're giving them a blueprint for what's possible in their own lives. And every interaction you have with a student—whether you're helping them navigate a challenging moment, celebrating their success, or simply modeling how to take a deep breath when things get overwhelming—plants a seed. You may never see the full fruit of that seed, but it grows. That student who watched you regulate your nervous system during a chaotic day in the classroom might use that same technique years later when they're facing their own stressful situation. The student who saw you set a kind but firm boundary when a demanding colleague tried to push back might remember that it's possible to say no with grace when they're an adult.

Teachers have shared incredible stories about the changes they've noticed since practicing the strategies in this book. They're responding instead of reacting to their students, fostering trust and stronger relationships. And their students are having more fun in their classes because they themselves are open to having more joy.

Abbie, an elementary school teacher, told me that her students are now asking for a reset if they need one, and they have even made it a habit to celebrate their own successes, "which is amazing in and of itself," she shared, "but I can tell it's also them more open to learning, too."

Leslie, an eighth-grade social studies teacher, finally recognized how her burnout was influencing the amount of time and energy she was pouring into her classroom and students. "These practices made it so I could be so much more available to my students," she told me. "I actually feel like a role model now that I'm not in a constant state of overwhelm."

Margaret felt more mindful and at peace with herself, which affected how she interacted with others. "I'm such a better communicator now," she shared. "I feel like I'm really connecting with people instead of just talking at them or letting their words slip past me." And through this work, Ben learned to accept that he is human and teaching is never going to be perfect. "But with that acceptance of myself and my students," he said, "I see that my students feel safer and more comfortable to learn, ask questions, and thrive!"

This is why this book is specifically for teachers, written from a holistic perspective, not just another general guide to navigating stress and burnout. Because when you do this work, you don't just transform your own life. You create a legacy that ripples out through every student whose life you touch, every colleague who witnesses your example, and every family member who benefits from your renewed energy and presence. You become part of breaking the cycle that keeps so many trapped in burnout, martyrdom, and emotional exhaustion even beyond the educational landscape.

The impact you make when you choose empowerment over sacrifice isn't just personal—it's generational and global. Transformative. More than worthy of celebration.

With that in mind, I'm going to be honest with you. In a few weeks, you're probably going to forget most of what you've read in this book. Grab your phone or a good old-fashioned analog calendar (yes, I still use one) and set a reminder for two weeks from today. Title it "Revisit *The Empowered Educator.*" And when that reminder pops up, actually come back to this book. Reengage with the work and recommit. Go through the exercises in these chapters. Celebrate. And share. You are a gift to this world. Act accordingly!

ACKNOWLEDGMENTS

In the spirit of this book, I first want to acknowledge myself. Yay ME! I did it! This book, which was once just a spark of an idea, is now in your hands! An unquenchable thirst for curiosity, a dash of confidence, and a healthy dose of delusion seemed to have been the perfect catalyst for this to grow. It feels magical to wholeheartedly believe in something that doesn't exist yet . . . and now here it is. With that said, this project was certainly not done in solitude. There are brilliant people behind the curtains who helped make all this possible, and for that, I am eternally grateful.

I want to first thank my editor, Lauren Appleton, and the team at Tarcher Perigee and Penguin Random House. You have been incredible throughout this whole experience. Meghan Stevenson, thank you for understanding my vision right away and believing in the importance of this message. When we first met, I knew I wanted to work with you, and a few years later, this idea for a book became a reality. Thank you, Claudia Gabel, for getting the ball rolling, and you, Blair Thornburgh, for your time, talent, and care in making this book come to life. Your "Blair flair" is second to none. It's been an absolute joy to work with you. To my agent, Trinity McFadden, thank you for your support throughout this entire process as this book came to fruition. I appreciate your guidance and partnership in this project.

To everyone in the Empowered Educator world, thank you! You are consistently inspiring me to do more and create a larger ripple effect further out into the world—thank you from the bottom of my heart. To my fantastic team, past and present, particularly Jillian, Kathleen, Lisa, Kristin, Paige, Renee, Liz, and Brooke, you are truly the best. This is all possible because of the way you show up every day.

Thank you to every one of my teachers, both in and out of the classroom. Special shout-outs to Carol McAmis, Tracy Litt, and Deborah Montgomery Cove, whose voice is in my mind often reminding me that I'm still just warming up. Thank you, Robyn, Molly, Kris, Jon, Janice, Juliet, Kelly, Otto, and Rachel, who are near and dear to my heart. You keep me laughing, grounded, and energetically ready for whatever comes next.

This book was written with the unwavering presence of Mom, Chuck, Dad, Mary, my sister, Rachel, and my brother-in-law, Mike. Your unconditional love and support have been the foundation from which I do everything. I've always believed in myself because you've always believed in me. Words cannot describe how grateful I am.

And finally, thank you to my children, Ethan and Sandra. You light up my world.

DISCUSSION QUESTIONS

1. What does it mean to be an empowered educator? How does that make a difference in school communities?

2. What happens to the way you lead, teach, and communicate when your nervous system is regulated? How does dysregulation show up in your interactions with students or colleagues?

3. What happens when you are aware of the subtle cues your body sends, and how do those signals influence others' sense of safety, motivation, and trust?

4. When you ask yourself why five times in a row, what deeper purpose or truth begins to reveal itself?

5. As you reflect on your current role, notice which aspects of your work still *light you up* (the moments that feel congruent with your deeper why.) Where, on the other hand, do you feel drained, dissonant, or out of sync with the educator you intended to be? What's on your *live with it/manage it/end it* lists?

6. When you slow down to notice your thoughts without judgment, what patterns or default narratives begin to surface? What happens when you practice the Thought Scan exercise?

7. How does the way you see yourself (as a teacher, leader, or caregiver) affect the ways you respond to your interactions throughout your day? What happens when you give yourself permission to be human first?

8. Think back to a time when things did not go well in your classroom. How could the Empowered Reflection questions help you transform those moments of frustration into growth?

9. What does advocacy look like in your current role, both for yourself and for others? Which type of advocacy (reactive, situational, or proactive) are you most comfortable with, and where do you want to do things differently?

10. When you listen closely to the way you speak to yourself, what patterns do you notice (especially in moments of stress or self-doubt)? How does that impact the way you go through your day?

11. How could your classroom or team culture evolve if everyone began to speak from awareness rather than autopilot?

12. When you intentionally create space to SHIFT (*sense, honor, integrate, focus,* and *transform*) before the week begins, what shifts in your emotional baseline or nervous system regulation do you notice? And how might this intentional start ripple outward, affecting your tone, your

decision-making, and the way your students or colleagues experience you on Monday morning?

13. What's one small shift you've made since reading this book that's created a noticeable ripple in your students, colleagues, or school culture?

14. Who are you now that you've given yourself permission to slow down, listen differently, and prioritize your well-being? In what ways has this book redefined how you see yourself as both an educator and a human being?

15. Knowing what you know now, how can you create a ripple effect in your school community?

NOTES

INTRODUCTION

1. Liz Riggs, "Why Do Teachers Quit? And Why Do They Stay?" *The Atlantic*, October 18, 2013. https://www.theatlantic.com/education/archive/2013/10/why-do-teachers-quit/280699/.

CHAPTER 3: DESIGN THE LIFE YOU'VE ALWAYS WANTED

1. Joe Dispenza, *Breaking the Habit of Being Yourself: How to Lose Your Mind and Create a New One* (Carlsbad, Calif.: Hay House, 2012).
2. Jason Murdock, "Humans Have More Than 6,000 Thoughts per Day, Psychologists Discover," *Newsweek*, July 15, 2020. https://www.newsweek.com/humans-6000-thoughts-every-day-1517963.
3. "REBT." The Albert Ellis Institute. https://albertellis.org/rebt-cbt-therapy.
4. Diana Nyad, "The Cuba Swim," DianaNyad.com, September 2, 2013. https://diananyad.com/the-cuba-swim.

CHAPTER 4: REWIRE YOUR BRAIN

1. Fowlers and Wells. *The American Phrenological Journal and Repository of Science, Literature and General Intelligence*, vols. 13–16 (New York: Fowlers and Wells, 1851), 89.
2. Stephen W. Porges, *The Polyvagal Theory: Neurophysiological Foundations of Emotions, Attachment, Communication, and Self-Regulation* (New York: W. W. Norton & Company, 2011).
3. Paul E. Dennison and Gail E. Dennison, *Brain Gym, Teacher's Edition Revised* (Ventura, CA: Edu-Kinesthetics, 1989).
4. Jill Bolte Taylor, *Whole Brain Living: The Anatomy of Choice and the Four Characters That Drive Our Life* (New York: Hay House, 2021).

5. Igor Branchi, "Plasticity in Mental Health: A Network Theory," *Neuroscience & Biobehavioral Reviews* 138 (2022): 104691. https://doi.org/10.1016/j.neubiorev.2022.104691.

CHAPTER 5: REFLECT TO REFRAME

1. John Tierney and Roy F. Baumeister, *The Power of Bad: How the Negativity Effect Rules Us and How We Can Rule It* (New York: Penguin Press, 2019).
2. Hammond, Zaretta. *Culturally Responsive Teaching and the Brain: Promoting Authentic Engagement and Rigor Among Culturally and Linguistically Diverse Students.* Corwin Press, 2015.

CHAPTER 7: SPEAK WITH INTENTION

1. Karim S. Kassam and Wendy Berry Mendes, "The Effects of Measuring Emotion: Physiological Reactions to Emotional Situations Depend on Whether Someone Is Asking," *PLoS One* 8, no. 6 (2013): e64959. https://www.ncbi.nlm.nih.gov/pmc/articles/PMC3680163/.
2. Katharina Kircanski, Matthew D. Lieberman, and Michelle G. Craske, "Feelings Into Words: Contributions of Language to Exposure Therapy." *Psychological Science* 23, no. 10 (2012): 1086–91. https://doi.org/10.1177/0956797612443830.
3. Jo Marchant, "Language Patterns Reveal Body's Hidden Response to Stress," *Nature,* 2017. https://doi.org/10.1038/nature.2017.22964.
4. Friedemann Pulvermüller, Yury Shtyrov, and Risto Ilmoniemi, "Brain Signatures of Meaning Access in Action Word Recognition," *Journal of Cognitive Neuroscience* 17, no. 6 (2005): 884–92. https://doi.org/10.1162/0898929054021111.
5. Paul H. Thibodeau and Lera Boroditsky, "Metaphors We Think With: The Role of Metaphor in Reasoning." *PLoS One* 6, no. 2 (2011): e16782. https://doi.org/10.1371/journal.pone.0016782.
6. Alexis Blue, "How the Brain Finds Meaning in Metaphor," Association of American Universities, April 11, 2019. https://www.aau.edu/research-scholarship/featured-research-topics/how-brain-finds-meaning-metaphor.
7. Terence D. Dores Cruz, Isabel Thielmann, Simon Columbus, et al., "Gossip and Reputation in Everyday Life." *Philosophical Transactions of the Royal Society B: Biological Sciences* 376, no. 1838 (2021): 20200301. https://doi.org/10.1098/rstb.2020.0301.
8. Shimul Melwani, *A Little Bird Told Me So . . . : The Emotional, Attributional, Relational, and Team-Level Outcomes of Engaging in Gossip,* PhD dissertation, University of Pennsylvania ProQuest Dissertations and Theses (244 pp.). https://www.proquest.com/openview/8606b4651a705f05419bcfaa5077d440/1.pdf.

9. Terence D. Dores Cruz, Bianca Beersma, Maria T. M. Dijkstra, and Myriam N. Bechtoldt, "The Bright and Dark Side of Gossip for Cooperation in Groups," *Frontiers in Psychology* 10 (June 20, 2019): Article 1374. https://doi.org/10.3389/fpsyg.2019.01374.
10. Elena Martinescu, Onne Janssen, and Bernard A. Nijstad, "Tell Me the Gossip: The Self-Evaluative Function of Receiving Gossip About Others." *Personality and Social Psychology Bulletin* 40, no. 12 (2014): 1668–80. https://doi.org/10.1177/0146167214554916.

CHAPTER 8: EXPERIENCE WELLNESS THAT LASTS

1. Terri Cole, "Breaking Free: The Intersection of Codependency and Over-Functioning in Relationships," TerriCole.com, April 11, 2019. https://www.terricole.com/codependency-over-functioning/.
2. Stephanie Marken and Sangeeta Agrawal, "K-12 Workers Have Highest Burnout Rate in U.S.," *Gallup News*, June 13, 2022. https://news.gallup.com/poll/393500/workers-highest-burnout-rate.aspx .
3. Joseph M. Kush, Elena Badillo-Goicoechea, Rashelle J. Musci, and Elizabeth A. Stuart, "Teacher Mental Health During the COVID-19 Pandemic," *Educational Researcher* 51, no. 9 (2022). https://doi.org/10.3102/0013189X221134281 .
4. Richard E. Boyatzis and Annie McKee, *Resonant Leadership: Renewing Yourself and Connecting with Others Through Mindfulness, Hope, and Compassion* (Boston: Harvard Business Review Press, 2005), 7.
5. Taylor, Jill Bolte. *My Stroke of Insight: A Brain Scientist's Personal Journey.* Viking, 2008.
6. Nagoski, Emily, and Amelia Nagoski. *Burnout: The Secret to Unlocking the Stress Cycle.* Ballantine Books, 2019.

CHAPTER 9: EXPAND YOUR IMPACT

1. Peter Salovey and John D. Mayer, "Emotional Intelligence," *Imagination, Cognition and Personality* 9, no. 3 (1990): 185–211. https://center.uoregon.edu/StartingStrong/uploads/STARTINGSTRONG2016/HANDOUTS/KEY_46201/pub153_SaloveyMayerICP1990_OCR.pdf.
2. Daniel Goleman, *Emotional Intelligence: Why It Can Matter More Than IQ* (New York: Bantam Books, 1995).
3. Alda, Alan. *If I Understood You, Would I Have This Look on My Face?: My Adventures in the Art and Science of Relating and Communicating.* Random House, 2017.

INDEX

ABOUT THE AUTHOR

Dr. Jen Rafferty is an educator, an author, a TEDx speaker, and the founder of Empowered Educator, an organization transforming the culture of education by placing educator well-being at the center of school success. She holds a PhD in educational psychology, degrees in music education and vocal performance, and certifications in Emotional Intelligence and Neuro-Identity Evolution. As a former middle school music teacher, Jen knows firsthand the challenges and joys of life in the classroom, and the toll it can take when personal well-being comes last. Her own journey from burnout to balance ignited her mission to help educators reconnect with their purpose, restore their energy, and feel empowered as leaders both in and out of the classroom.